SUPERNATURAL™

THE OFFICIAL COMPANION
SEASON 5

SUPERNATURAL:
THE OFFICIAL COMPANION SEASON 5
ISBN 9781848567399

Published by
Titan Books
A division of Titan Publishing Group Ltd
144 Southwark Street, London SE1 0UP

First edition October 2010
2 4 6 8 10 9 7 5 3 1

Visit our website:
www.titanbooks.com

DEDICATION
Dedicated to my brother-in-law Ken and my mother-in-law Agnes, who have assisted me in ways beyond measure.

ACKNOWLEDGEMENTS
Endless thanks are given to all the people who helped make this book a reality. First and foremost, to Eric Kripke and everyone who graciously gave up their limited time to be interviewed; Kim Dainard, Rebecca Dessertine, Jason Fischer, Brigitta Fry, Jenny Klein, Marc Klein, and Holly Ollis for their tireless coordination; Chris Cooper, Christine Donovan, Lee Anne Elaschuk, Ivan Hayden, Adrian Hrytzak, Mary-Ann Liu, and Jerry Wanek for the visual materials; Sandy Auden and the helpful teams of MCM Expo Group and Rogue Events, especially Wayne Munn, for implementing additional interviews; my family for their steadfast support; and to my editors, Jo Boylett at Titan Books and Christopher Cerasi at DC Comics, who are always a pleasure to work with.

Titan Books would like to thank the cast and crew of *Supernatural*, in particular Eric Kripke, and Sera Gamble for the Foreword. Our thanks also to Christopher Cerasi at DC Comics for all his help, and to Christine Donovan at Warner Bros.

To receive advance information, news, competitions, and exclusive Titan offers online, please register as a member by clicking the "sign up" button on our website: **www.titanbooks.com** Did you enjoy this book? We love to hear from our readers. Please e-mail us at: **readerfeedback@titanemail.com** or write to Reader Feedback at the above address.

SUPERNATURAL

THE OFFICIAL COMPANION
SEASON 5

Supernatural created by Eric Kripke

NICHOLAS KNIGHT

TITAN BOOKS

CONTENTS

FOREWORD

So, the Apocalypse was a blast.

Okay, not so much for Sam. He had that planet of guilt about having inadvertently brought the whole damn thing on. Or Dean, so overwhelmed by his presumed destiny that at one point he was ready to chuck it all in. Or Bobby, who lost the use of his legs. Or Castiel, whose angel mojo ran out. Or, you know, all those characters we killed.

So, actually, the only people who had fun were the writers. We got to unleash Lucifer, and the Four Horsemen, and the Whore of Babylon. Also a very cute little anti-Christ. We got to go to Heaven. We got to save the world.

How we did this: Eric Kripke came in with this crazy, bold vision, which basically amounted to, "Hey, guys, let's freakin' *do the Apocalypse.*" Then he worked tirelessly, juggling so much crap in his head that it's now obvious to me that he's a replicant.

The rest of us — that'd be Bob Singer (who has also directed some of the coolest episodes of the series), Ben Edlund, Jeremy Carver, Andrew Dabb, Dan Loflin, Julie Siege, and me — got in the writers' room and went... well, kinda nuts. Because we *got to do the Apocalypse.* I mean, shows threaten the Apocalypse all the time, but generally, they avert it by the end of the season. Some of my favorite shows made a point of averting it *every* season. But it's not often you see a show just... go for it.

Did we pull it off? That's for you to judge. But I will say: in my humble estimation, we did some of our ballsiest episodes this season. By far our most ambitious. Many of our directors (Phil Sgriccia, who is also our post-production supervisor, leaps to mind) did their finest work. Jensen and Jared and Misha and Jim and our shockingly classy list of guest stars blew everybody's mind. And yeah, there are a couple of stories in there we wish we could do over. A few moments we wish we had the blockbuster-movie money to do onscreen instead of off, or big instead of small. Also: seriously, if only you got to experience the dialogue we actually come up with in the

writers' room. Unfortunately, it's completely unfit for network TV. But the versions of Sam and Dean that live in our minds, before we scrub 'em down? Positively poetic in their use of the expletive.

By the way, before I go — which I have to do, because we're deep into season *six* now, believe it or not — let me explain exactly how we keep pulling the wacky trick of getting renewed. Two factors.

Number one: you. It's because you showed up and watched. And told your friends. And jumped on the internet. And praised us and bitched us out and generally became one of the strongest and most passionate fandoms ever.

Number two: our team. All told, it takes well over three hundred people to make *Supernatural*. They are the hardworking yet eerily pleasant crew that shoots the show in Vancouver. They build the sets, sturdily enough to bear all six-feet-whatever of Jared Padalecki ratcheting into the walls. They costume our zombies. Computer-generate our demon smoke. Dress every motel. Make sure no one drops a line. Put out casting calls for Indian goddesses. Scout the creepiest locations. Operate the technocrane. Choreograph endless variations on the direction "Sam fights the bad guy." Light the alleyway. Paint the bruises on Jensen. Grab the coffee. (Trust me, without the people who get the coffee, this whole thing would get ugly quick.)

So, thanks to them. And thanks to you. I hope you enjoyed the end of the world as much as we did.

Sera Gamble
July 2010

Above

Dean (Jensen Ackles) and Sam (Jared Padalecki), about to have an unexpected reunion with some old friends, in 'Good God, Y'all', written by Sera Gamble.

INTENSIFYING SUPERNATURAL

DEAN: Screw the angels and the demons and their crap Apocalypse. They want to fight a war, they can find their own planet. This one's ours, and I say they get the hell of it. We take 'em all on. We kill the Devil. Hell, we even kill Michael if we have to. But we do it our own damn selves

"In season five we found ourselves at the climax of a five-year storyline, and the show became much more challenging to produce," explains creator Eric Kripke. "I almost dare say we bit off more than we could chew, but you gotta give us credit for trying to take big bites. It's one thing when you're in season one to say, 'Yeah, this sucker's going to end with the Apocalypse!' It's another thing entirely to actually have to find a way to mount and execute a twenty-two episode Apocalypse on our time and budget. But I think we did the absolute best we could have given our situation. I'm really pleased with how the story of the mythology wraps up — we had some great episodes this season."

One of the hardest parts of creating the Apocalypse for TV was coming up with suitable stories to do it justice. "This year was far and away the hardest year of *Supernatural* for me," Kripke states. He spent even more time than usual in the writers' room trying to break the story and answer difficult questions like, "'What is God's motivation? What is the Devil's motivation? What are the Horsemen like, and what do they want? Exactly what does this Apocalypse look like and how do we give it the appropriate scope while still being able to produce it for a budget?' It was such an incredibly difficult year figuring all that stuff out," he says. "This was a year where breaking the story in many ways felt like being in a quarry breaking rocks, where you're just slowly but surely plodding through and making progress step by step."

Fortunately, there were no rocks left unbroken, and in the end, Kripke says, "I think it played out exactly the way we were counting on it to. I just wish we'd had more money to do it with [an] epic scope. Our Apocalypse had a very specific focus on details and phenomenon — this small thing happened here and this small event happened there — and I would've liked to have had more episodes like 'The End', in which it was like the doors were blown off. 'The End' was a huge episode, and it really made it feel like the world was coming to an end, but the production challenge was pretty significant, and you can't sustain that over twenty-two episodes. You can't have twenty-two episodes with people running around flailing their arms, saying, 'It's the end of the world!' So we had to adopt this notion, which I think worked, that says, 'Well, who's to say the Apocalypse isn't going on right now all around us? Who's to say that swine flu and hurricanes and floods and earthquakes and massive oil spills off the coast of the United States aren't the signs of the Apocalypse right now?'" After all, a world in which people are going to their jobs and going about their

DID YOU KNOW?

On why *Supernatural* hit the one hundredth episode milestone, executive producer McG says, "I think it's because *Supernatural* has a really original voice." Regardless of how many more episodes the show produces, McG declares, "It's always going to have a soft spot in my heart."

lives while there's a secret war going on is how it's always been on *Supernatural*.

Ultimately, Kripke's very happy with the way the five-year arc ended. "It was fun and gratifying for it to end the way I really always wanted it to," he says. "I always loved the idea that you have this very epic, highfalutin prophecy about chosen ones and end times, and then you have this blue-collar guy, who's American and stubborn and cocky, walk up to it and say, 'Prophecy is for wussies. Go to Hell!' and kick it in the ass; just totally puncture it. I always wanted it to end that way. There's this massive prophecy and it just ends with Dean playing Def Leppard and riding the Impala up to Michael and Lucifer. There they are on the chosen battlefield, and Dean drives onto it and calls one of them 'Buttercup' and he tells the other one that he wants five minutes to talk with the son-of-a-bitch. Putting a cowboy in the middle of *The Lord of the Rings* is something I've always really wanted to do, because that

WISHFUL THINKING

During the filming of season five, the cast and crew spent a day with a young Australian girl suffering from cancer. For her, it was literally a wish come true, thanks to the Make-A-Wish Foundation. "Jared Padalecki and Jensen Ackles were so touched by the time they spent with her," says Kim Dainard, assistant to producer Jim Michaels. "When she left, the guys pulled me aside and asked me to bring forward some ideas for raising money for the foundation, because Make-A-Wish is pretty incredible."

Above

Castiel's (Misha Collins) search for God intensifies as the Apocalypse draws near.

Opposite

Sam and Dean don't know which way to turn on this highway in Heaven.

stuff is a little self-important, so you inflate the self-importance of it and then you immediately deflate it by saying, 'Yeah, but that crap ain't American.' That was the vibe I've always been enamored with and the way I really wanted it to be.

"Now that it's all said and done in terms of the run of my storyline on *Supernatural*, people can see that it was what it always was; it's the same story it was before there were angels. There's humanity and a bunch of supernatural sons-of-bitches that are screwing with humanity, and humanity will always win. It's not about prophecy, it's not about destiny, it's about saving the guy next to you in the foxhole. It's about simple honesty and the dignity of human nature. All of these highfalutin creatures, whether they're angels or demons, can suck it! Right from season one there was a vibe that it was these two blue-collar guys against the supernatural, and I was very gratified that after going into all this prophecy I was able to get back to what I thought the point of the show was."

One thing Kripke hadn't planned right from season one though was making God an actual character on the show. "No," he agrees, "there was never really a plan for that. I always knew there was going to be the Devil and that that's what Sam's destiny was, and Sam was going to start the Apocalypse. But I never really thought about the other side of the coin, and that's what angels gave us. Then with angels, once it gets bigger, it just inevitably leads to God.

"Specifically, the notion of God in season five came out of the initial conversations we had for this season about giving Castiel his own quest and making it feel like it was an important part of the core mythology. I was a big fan of the comic book series *Preacher*, as were a couple of other writers in the room, and it's always been tonally one of the influences for *Supernatural*, and the core story of *Preacher* is this guy who is on a quest to find God and basically make Him answer for His sins. We always liked that idea, so we said, 'Since it's the Apocalypse, why not have one of our characters, Cass, look for God?' Since God is Castiel's father, and in season one Sam and Dean were on a search for their father, it makes sense that in season five it all comes full circle with another one of our characters searching for their father. So we said, 'Okay, let's make God a character. Let's go for it.' I think we were kind of smitten with the recklessness of it, and we had this attitude of 'Let's be as bold and risky as we can, and if we fall flat on our face, then so be it.' Which we probably did once or twice, but no one can accuse us of playing it safe…"

No one could accuse them of taking the easy road, either. "Whenever we were sitting in the [writers'] room trying to suss out God's motivation in any particular scene, we started giggling to ourselves," Kripke relates, "because we were like, 'Gossip Girl does not have this problem! The writers' room of 90210 is not sitting around debating the conflicting philosophies of fate versus free will.'" As Heaven's gardener, Joshua, says in 'Dark Side of the Moon', "You could drive yourself nuts asking questions like that." But they did anyway.

Kripke continues, "We were asking questions like, 'Where does God stand on all of this? Is the universe just one massive test for humanity?' I was proud of our little

THE SUPERNATURAL IMPALAS

To help celebrate Supernatural's hundredth episode, an all-Supernatural band, The Impalas, got together and played at the party. "There are a couple of guys on set who are musicians, and we talked about music a lot," recalls executive producer Robert Singer. "We felt it'd be cool to put a band together of people who work on the show. The first time we got together, it was just to see if it would work, and we said, 'You know what? This is pretty good!' Then it became, 'Yeah, we're gonna do this!' There was a lot of trepidation about how we'd be received, but the crowd at the party was really receptive to us, and we had a great time."

There's even a possibility that the show's fans will get to see The Impalas. Maybe at a Supernatural convention? "That'd be fun," Singer says. "We're open to it."

Above

Sam needs Chuck (Rob Benedict) to stall for time with the fans so he and Dean can save innocent lives.

show, that those were the questions we were asking in the writers' room, but those are intimidating questions to ask when we're just a bunch of TV writers trying to make a horror show. Philosophers have been wrestling with those concepts for thousands of years and still haven't come up with a satisfactory answer, so who are we to try to answer those questions? We just did our own *Supernatural* take on it and tried our best to make it entertaining."

On a show that had already featured several other gods, it makes sense that, once God and the Devil started stirring things up with the Apocalypse, those other gods would be a little concerned, to say the least. "The idea that a bunch of gods can be living undercover in the United States comes from Neil Gaiman's *American Gods*," Kripke reveals. "*American Gods* has always been a major influence on the tone of *Supernatural* and its storylines, so we owe Neil Gaiman a huge debt of gratitude. Actually, though, it was David Reed, our script coordinator, who had the idea of, 'Why don't they all have a convention and talk about the Apocalypse?' So it really sprung from that. We were inspired by that, and we were really interested in the notion we'd been talking about all season, in which we were saying, 'This is a really Christian Apocalypse — wouldn't the other religions have something to say about it?' It was always sort of bothering us, and finally we were able to have the episode ['Hammer of the Gods'] where we could address that."

As always, in season five, gods, demons, and assorted other supernatural creatures took a backseat to the central story of Sam and Dean Winchester. "Last season Sam and Dean kind of split up, then this season they came back together as brothers," Kripke points out. "It happened in dribs and drabs, and we intentionally did that

LIGHTS, CAMERAS, LAUGHTER

Stunt Coordinator Lou Bollo gives us a glimpse of Jared Padalecki and Jensen Ackles' antics on the *Supernatural* set when the cameras aren't rolling. "They're so playful," he says. "The best time to watch them play around is during a rehearsal. They've been told by the director what he'd like to see, and instead they come out and give the funniest version of that scene you've ever seen. Like, if it's just jumping over a fence and going inside a window, they'll look like the clumsiest guys on the face of the Earth, trying to scramble up the fence, falling backward, and trying to help each other up. They'll look like a couple of complete goofs. The director will just go, 'Oh, God...' but everybody gets a good laugh. Then when the cameras roll, it's all perfect. It's so funny."

Above

Dean and Bobby (Jim Beaver) decipher exactly what "In a castle on a hill made of 42 dogs" means.

Above

Archangel Michael
(Matt Cohen)
saves young Mary
Winchester (Amy
Gumenick) from rogue
angel Anna (Julie
McNiven).

because that's how we thought real relationships went. At first Dean couldn't forgive Sam, and then they were back together, and then even when they were together, tensions resurfaced. Then finally both brothers had to just grow up.

"Sam had to truly overcome his addiction and darkness and really face in many ways what it meant — not just solving the symptoms, but solving the problem, which in our minds was that the anger came from self-hatred, because he always felt like a freak. He'd been calling himself a freak since season one, and finally he had to get over that and do the right thing, and be strong even though he was facing all this terrible temptation. We were talking about Sam's story this season in many ways as the story of a recovering addict. You try to get back to your family and they're angry at you and don't trust you, and you need support and sometimes you get it and sometimes you don't. You're battling valiantly against the demons that are trying to seduce you back

APOCALYPSE NOW

Jensen Ackles shares his views on the way the five-year arc ended. "I liked it!" he exclaims. "I'm really proud of Eric Kripke, and proud to be associated with a show that didn't go against what it'd originally planned to do. He had a five-year story planned out from the get-go, and I think the fact that he stuck to it, that he didn't try to stretch a five-year storyline over six years or more and fill the gaps with a bunch of fluff, that he wrapped up what he'd started the way he'd intended to wrap it up, shows a lot of character. "Some might be concerned that that might not leave us anywhere to go, but having the writing team that we do, I'm sure they've been thinking about 'Where do we go from here?' for a couple seasons, and they've got ideas piling up."

Above

Lucifer (Mark
Pellegrino) tells Sam
that he wants to wear
his meatsuit to the
Apocalypse — and
perhaps forever.

into your old life — in an addict's case, figuratively, in Sam's case, literally.

"Dean had to really grow up in his own way too," Kripke continues. "He had to acknowledge that Sam isn't all freak and that his brother really isn't the snot-nosed kid that he's had to keep on the straight-and-narrow. Dean had to both forgive Sam in a way and acknowledge that it wasn't an older brother-little brother relationship anymore, that they were both truly equals. By the end of the season, I think he did that. The main reason he signed off on the Lucifer plan in the first place was that he decided that for better or for worse he had to back Sam's play and trust him.

"I think this was a season in which both brothers took substantial moves in maturing and learning how to have a more functional relationship at the end of it all," Kripke concludes. "Unfortunately, Sam dove into Hell just when they were about ready to figure their crap out — but such is the world of *Supernatural*." 🖉

BROTHER VS BROTHER

Onscreen, the angels wanted Sam and Dean — as vessels for Lucifer and Michael — to face off against each other, but what would happen if Jared Padalecki and Jensen Ackles got into a no-holds-barred fight in real life? "That's an interesting question," muses stunt coordinator Lou Bollo. "Oh, it'd be messy. Jared's probably the stronger of the two of them — he is really powerful. We've gotten into some play fights and it wasn't good for me at all. But Jensen is very fast. He's so quick — you can't believe how fast this guy is! Our stunt guys can't outrun him when they're trying to chase him down the street to tackle him. They can't even get close to him because he gets going and is like, 'Well, I'm only going half-speed.' Jared and Jensen are buddies, though, so they wouldn't fight each other. They get along really, really well."

ZACHARIAH: What, you thought you could *actually* kill Lucifer?

SEASON 5 REGULAR CAST:

Main
Jared Padalecki (Sam Winchester)
Jensen Ackles (Dean Winchester)
Misha Collins (Castiel)

Recurring
Jim Beaver (Bobby Singer)
Mark Pellegrino (Nick/Lucifer)
Rob Benedict (Chuck Shurley)
Kurt Fuller (Zachariah)
Mark Sheppard (Crowley)

SYMPATHY FOR THE DEVIL

Written by:
Eric Kripke

Directed by:
Robert Singer

Guest Cast: Rachel Miner (Meg), Emily Perkins (Becky Rosen), Mark Burgess (Father Joe), Marci T. House (Nurse), Frank Topol (Pilot), Bellamy Young (Sarah/Lucifer)

The door to Lucifer's cage opens, unleashing a bright light and a deafening noise that brings Sam and Dean to their knees. Then they suddenly find themselves safely aboard an airplane. They head to Chuck's house, where Dean left Castiel, but Chuck breaks the news that the archangel that was protecting him smote Castiel. Zachariah arrives, but Dean uses an Enochian blood sigil to send him away.

In Pike Creek, Delaware, strange things are happening to a man named Nick, and he's seeing things too — including a woman covered in blood, who tells him he's been chosen...

Chuck, who is being watched by angels, has his number one fan, Becky, take a message to the boys: "The Michael Sword is on Earth. The angels lost it. In a castle. On a hill made of forty-two dogs." The brothers bring in Bobby for help deciphering Chuck's message, but Dean realizes that the Michael Sword is in his father's storage locker. But Bobby has been possessed by a demon and attacks Dean. The demon Meg arrives and orders Bobby to kill Dean, but Bobby regains control and stabs himself with the demon-killing knife. Dean retrieves the knife but Meg smokes out.

The Winchesters leave Bobby at a hospital and race to Buffalo, New York, where they find dead demon meatsuits in the storage unit. Zachariah is there with angel goons. He tells them Dean is the Michael Sword — the archangel's destined vessel. Dean refuses to say yes to Michael, so Zachariah breaks Sam's legs, gives Dean stomach cancer, then removes Sam's lungs. A very much alive Castiel then arrives and kills the other angels. Zachariah doesn't understand how Cass is alive, so he fixes the brothers and vanishes. Castiel carves an Enochian sigil into Sam and Dean's ribs, hiding them from angels.

Lucifer appears to Nick in a dream, in the form of Nick's dead wife, and asks the man to be his vessel. Lucifer likens his own "betrayal" by God to Nick's, when God "allowed" Nick's wife and child to be murdered by an intruder. Lucifer tells Nick that he wants to hold God accountable for His actions.

The brothers visit Bobby in hospital, and discover that the doctors told Bobby he will probably never walk again. Outside, Dean tells Sam he doesn't think he can trust him. Meanwhile, Nick says yes to Lucifer...

ZACHARIAH: You're *the* vessel. Michael's vessel.
DEAN: How? Why... why me?
ZACHARIAH: Because you're *chosen!* It's a great honor, Dean.
DEAN: Oh, yeah. Life as an angel condom. That's real fun.
I think I'll pass, thanks.

DID YOU KNOW?

During a scene where Kurt Fuller is face-to-face with Jensen Ackles, Jared Padalecki got hold of a can of compressed air (which the camera people use to blow dust off the lenses). "He was sticking the nozzle up my pant leg and blasting me with air," Fuller reveals.

Above

Meg (Rachel Miner) and a demon-possessed Bobby catch Dean by surprise.

You would think the Devil would be used to hot places, what with the whole fire and brimstone thing. However, the actor who plays him for most of season five hasn't been similarly acclimatized, and almost got heatstroke during shooting. "I had to work in Vancouver during the hottest days that they ever had in recorded history," states Pellegrino. "I was put up in an apartment that had no air-conditioning, and by the time I got in it was like 115 degrees in there. It was horrendous. I stayed out until eleven o'clock at night and it was still a sauna."

Along with Lucifer's appearance in 'Sympathy for the Devil', another of Hell's denizens makes a surprise return to Earth to torment the Winchesters — Meg. One of the first things she did when she got out of Hell was kiss Dean. Despite what some of the fans might think about kissing Jensen Ackles, though, Rachel Miner is adamant that there was nothing hot about their kiss. "I hate to disappoint, but kisses and love scenes in film are usually not in the least romantic. You try to make it look that way, but it's so technical. You're mostly thinking about timing and making sure you're not blocking the other person or the camera. And, no," Miner adds, "I did not eat peanut butter before the kiss. I don't usually eat garlic and chug coffee right before, either."

Above

Demon-Bobby waits for the right moment to strike.

Sam would probably have preferred if Meg had kissed him too, instead of kicking his butt. "I love doing that stuff," Miner enthuses. "I do my own stunts whenever possible. There's something very invigorating about getting to kick some butt, even if it's pretend. Plus, the stunt coordinator on the show, Lou Bollo, is awesome."

BECKY: Yes, I'm a fan, but I really don't appreciate being mocked. I know that _Supernatural_ is just a book, okay? I know the difference between fantasy and reality.
CHUCK: Becky, it's all real.
BECKY: I knew it!

The show's producers think Miner is pretty awesome, too. "I thought she really acted the role terrifically," says executive producer Robert Singer. "And she had this aura of evil about her that was kind of scary." What would have been really scary is if they had hired a less talented actress to take over the role. "Definitely," agrees creator Eric Kripke. "In rebooting Meg, we really wanted to pay credit to Nicki Aycox, the original Meg. In fact, we spent a lot of time in the writers' room trying to figure out how to bring Meg back in Aycox's meatsuit because we loved the actress so much, but we went to so much trouble having her die and disposing of the corpse, and it's been rotting in the ground for four years, and then we wiped out Meg Masters' soul in season four... We just couldn't figure out why Meg the

MUSIC

'Thunderstruck' by AC/DC

Above

Meg is the last
person Sam
expected to find in
his motel room.

demon would dig up a rotting body and reanimate it, versus just picking a new victim. So the bar was set very high, because we needed someone who had Nicki's chops. The casting process is always taxing, but Rachel Miner walked in the door and was just so interesting and complicated and sexy and idiosyncratic. There are so many different layers to her. I think she carries on Meg's mantel quite nicely."

It's too bad the Prophet Chuck didn't foresee Bobby being possessed by Meg's minion in time to save Bobby, but he was a little distracted, what with having Castiel's remains splattered all over his house. Chuck was a little jumpy, too, which led him to take a swing at Sam. "I had to shoot swinging the plunger at Sam several times so we could get it right," reveals Rob Benedict. "Moments like that are really hard to shoot because you can't really hit him. But I think a couple of times I actually did hit Jared in the face. It was a really soft fake plunger, but still… We had to shoot that several times because after I hit him in the face I was trying not to [again], and you could tell I wasn't hitting him. That was fun, though."

The introduction of Chuck's number one fan, Becky Rosen, was also fun. "The scene where I go into the motel room where the boys are hanging out was kind of nerve-wracking," says Emily Perkins. "But she's such a forward character, and I'm a pretty shy person, so it was cool to play someone like that." In fact, Perkins enjoyed it a little *too* much at first. "Bob told me to hold back a little more from how excited I was in the first few takes," she says. "I overplayed it a little bit and then he was like, 'Okay, you don't need to go *that* far.'"

DID YOU KNOW?

If Jim Beaver was possessed by a demon for real, he doesn't think he could regain control like Bobby did. "Are you kidding?" he asks. "I can't even get my kid to brush her teeth!"

GOOD GOD, Y'ALL

Written by: Sera Gamble

Directed by: Phil Sgriccia

Guest Cast: Samantha Ferris (Ellen Harvelle), Alona Tal (Jo Harvelle), Shawn Roberts (Austin), Genevieve Fleming (Kimberly), Michael Bean (Pastor), Josh Young (Kimberly's Husband), Autumn Bri Shadd (Teenaged Girl), Steve Love (Teenaged Boy), Steven Williams (Rufus Turner), Titus Welliver (Roger/War)

Stuck in a wheelchair, Bobby is angry when he discovers that Castiel, who is cut off from Heaven, can't heal him. Castiel is angry, too, since he rebelled for the boys and they failed to prevent Lucifer's release from Hell. He tells them they can't kill Lucifer, but he plans to find God using Dean's amulet, which burns hot in God's presence.

A call from Rufus brings Sam and Dean to River Pass, Colorado, a town infested by demons. The brothers are greeted by Ellen, who splashes holy water in Dean's face, then slaps him for not keeping in touch. Jo and Rufus are missing, and Ellen is protecting some of the surviving townsfolk. The Winchesters go for supplies, and after killing two demons, Sam is tempted to lick his knife. Sam and Ellen eventually find Jo and Rufus, but they are possessed by demons, and they take Sam captive. Strangely, they act like normal humans and treat Sam like he's a demon.

A local man tells Sam he is one of the Four Horsemen of the Apocalypse: War. He's giving everyone hallucinations, making them fight each other. When Dean learns that Jo thought Ellen was possessed, he checks the Bible and realizes that the omens that brought Rufus to town were actually signs of the Horseman's arrival. War makes everyone think Dean and Ellen are demons, but they escape and get to Sam and the others in time to stop a complete massacre. Still, the townsfolk continue attacking each other until Sam and Dean grab War and cut off his power source — a magical ring. Later, Sam tells Dean that he has realized he has to stop hunting and stay away from demon blood. Dean doesn't argue, so they go their separate ways.

CASTIEL: Your plan... to *kill Lucifer*—
DEAN: Yeah, you wanna help?
CASTIEL: No. It's *foolish*. It can't be done.
DEAN: Oh, well thanks for the support.

In 'Good God, Y'all' we finally find out the significance of Dean's amulet, which Jensen Ackles had been wearing since the Pilot. "It's kind of funny," Ackles says, "the amulet never really had a definitive purpose starting out. In choosing Dean's look in the very beginning, Eric Kripke and I agreed that Dean would have accoutrements about him; things that he'd picked up along the way — medallions or trinkets to ward off ghosts or to keep his soul intact and all that stuff. Maybe witch doctors gave

him something when he was down in the bayou, or whatever it might be. I wanted things about him that made it look like he'd traveled around a little bit, which is why he wore the bracelet and the rings and had an amulet around his neck. Then the writers built the story that the amulet came from Sam at an early age, which I thought was cool, because it gave it some purpose. When it came to fruition as far as what it meant and what its purpose actually was, I thought that was great."

As it turns out though, Ackles was happy to throw it away. "That thing was heavy!" he says. "It's a solid piece of brass. I would forget to change it out with the rubberized one every now and again when I was doing stunts, and I've lost little chips of my teeth from the horns hitting my mouth. After four seasons of wearing it around my neck, I'm kind of glad to get rid of it."

Ackles was almost stuck with the amulet for all of season five and possibly longer. "We had an earlier version [of the 'Good God, Y'all' plot] where we had another amulet that was the God-finding amulet," reveals executive producer Sera Gamble. "But we'd talked about the special significance of Dean's amulet for a long time, and we'd written to it, like in the flashback scene where we explain how Dean first got the

DID YOU KNOW?

When Sam and Dean are first walking through River Pass, there is a banner advertising "Pioneer Days" on which production designer Jerry Wanek is featured as the Grand Marshall alongside "Rodeo Queen Lee Lee Laschuk" (a.k.a. graphic artist Lee Anne Elaschuk).

Above

Dean and Sam contemplate whether the inhabitants of the deserted town have all gone on up to the 'Spirit in the Sky'.

MUSIC

'Long, Long Way From Home' by Foreigner

'Spirit in the Sky' by Norman Greenbaum

amulet. We had a discussion back then about how we could later do an episode about its special powers, and then this opportunity came up to get more specific about what those powers could be." Fortunately for Ackles, they decided that using that other God-finding amulet "just wasn't as cool."

Another thing Gamble finds cool about this episode is that "there is sort of a zombie vibe to an entire town of people getting possessed by demons." Executive producer Phil Sgriccia latched on to that vibe to make the zombie-demon-brainwashed-townsfolk good and creepy. "Phil was directing, and he always loves to have a good time," notes Jared Padalecki. "He really loves to work hard and play hard!"

For this episode, Sgriccia also got to work with Samantha Ferris and Alona Tal again. "It was so good to have them back because they're topnotch actors," he says. "I had the good fortune of being the one that directed them to begin with [in 'Everybody Loves a Clown'] a few seasons back, so it was wonderful to see them again. It's always fun to bring back people we like, and we like those two a lot. We had a good time with them."

Tal and Ferris had a good time as well, and Ferris particularly "had a blast" throwing holy water in Ackles' face. "That wasn't even my idea," she says. "I wish I could say it was." It wasn't Ferris's idea to slap Jensen for real, either, but she admits, "Yeah, I did hit him once. Not hard; I think I got him with the tips of my fingers. Jensen said everything's happened to him. Over the last five years he's been kicked and punched, he and Jared have hurt themselves and hurt each other."

Ferris had to be careful not to hurt Tal too, when her on-screen daughter was treating her like an evil skank. "That [fighting] stuff was fun," Ferris recalls, "but it was a smoking hot summer day." At least they didn't have the added difficulty of fighting with the limited visibility that comes from wearing black contact lenses. "It was a CGI thing, so we had to imagine each others' eyes were demon black."

CASTIEL: This is not a *theological* issue, it's *strategic*. With God's help, we can *win*.
DEAN: It's a pipedream, Cass.
CASTIEL: I killed two angels this week. Those are my *brothers*. I'm *hunted*. I *rebelled*. And I did it, all of it, for *you* — and you *failed*. You and your brother *destroyed the world*. And I lost *everything* — for *nothing*. So keep your opinions to yourself.

For visual effects supervisor Ivan Hayden and his crew, demon eyes are a snap, but snapping a bridge in half, now there's a challenge. "The bridge shot in 'Good God, Y'all' was a great one," enthuses Hayden. "We did it in just four days. A lot of times when we're filming stuff like that, the crew's looking at us like, 'How the hell are you going to do that?' and we have to figure out exactly how we're going to pull it together in time." They did, though, and Hayden loves the way it turned out. "When the boys come across the bridge, you don't see that coming, you look at it and go, 'Wow!'" ✍

Below
The brothers run into an old friend, but she doesn't seem very pleased to see them at first.

FREE TO BE YOU AND ME

Written by:
Jeremy Carver

Directed by:
J. Miller Tobin

Guest Cast: Demore Barnes (Donnie Finnerman/Raphael), Colin Lawrence (Reggie Hull), Sean Campbell (Steve Bose), Murray Lowry (Al), Katya Virshilas (Chastity), Ed Welch (Vampire), Peter Bryant (Deputy Walt Framingham), Ted Cole (Doctor), Michelle Simick (TV Reporter), Adrianne Palicki (Jessica), Emma Bell (Lindsey), Scott Michael Campbell (Tim Janklow)

Sam and Dean are now leading separate lives. Dean is hunting vampires in Greeley, Pennsylvania, while Sam is bussing tables at a bar in Garber, Oklahoma. Sam sees Revelation omens of hail and fire, but he calls Bobby and gets him to send other hunters. Meanwhile, Castiel pops in on Dean and asks for his help in capturing Raphael, the archangel who killed him.

In a dream, Sam talks with his dead girlfriend, Jessica. She says he shouldn't run away from hunting because people around him will die anyway, but he's convinced things will be different this time. Three hunters arrive because of Sam's tip and get jumped by ten demons, who inform them that Sam started the Apocalypse. Two of the hunters survive and go after Sam, threatening to kill his new friend Lindsey if he doesn't drink some demon blood and use his powers to get revenge on the demons. Sam fights them off, but is clearly rattled.

In Waterville, Maine, Castiel and Dean locate a vessel Raphael deserted, and Castiel is confident he can bring Raphael back with a ritual at dawn, but the odds are against Castiel surviving. Dean doesn't want Castiel to die a virgin, but they get kicked out of the whorehouse Dean takes them to when Cass psychoanalyzes a hooker. Their ploy to trap Raphael with Holy Fire works, but the archangel claims God is dead. Castiel still believes God is alive, so Dean tells him to keep looking. Dean also says he feels good not having to worry about his brother.

Jessica appears to Sam again, but she is really Lucifer in disguise. Lucifer reveals that Sam is his true vessel and is certain that Sam will eventually say yes to him.

CASTIEL: This is a den of iniquity. I should not be here.
DEAN: Dude, you full-on rebelled against Heaven. Iniquity is one of the perks!

DID YOU KNOW?

Colin Lawrence also played Jason in 'Faith'. Katya Virshilas also played Lust in 'The Magnificent Seven'.

Not since season one's 'Scarecrow' have Sam and Dean split up and been so geographically distant from each other as they are in 'Free to Be You and Me' (not counting the time they spent apart when Dean was in Hell). It's a significant moment in the brothers' relationship and in the show's story arc, which is why the producers wanted to get the mood of the teaser just right. "We tried out a lot of songs for that

opening montage," says editor Nicole Baer, "but Lynyrd Skynyrd's 'Simple Man' definitely conveyed the right mood and had the right lyrics."

"We had some pretty long conversations about the parallel tracks and what that meant for each of them," says director J. Miller Tobin. "It's written very deliberately in the sense that the whole opening teaser is the two of them in their parallel lives. It's specifically written to contrast between Sam being a barback and Dean still continuing to hunt, which I really loved."

Stunt coordinator Lou Bollo didn't love Sam being a barback, at least, not during filming. "It was super hot, and we were stuck in that ratty old bar. It was pretty horrible working in those conditions. But we had a lot of fun doing that fight between Sam and the other hunters. We had a real pool table in there, and we were slamming people down onto the slate. Of course, right away, Jared's gotta get involved in that. He just loves that kind of stuff, the same with Jensen. There were guys going over the table and hitting the floor, with not a lot of opportunity to even put pads down for them, at least for the stunt guys. Jared and Jensen are like a couple of kids — they've *got to* get involved in this stuff, they just love playing around with it, as long as they feel in their heads that they're not putting production at risk by getting hurt.

"That was a hellish couple of days in there," Bollo continues. "It was the heat-wave of the century. It was crazy. I bought an air conditioner for my trailer so I could sleep."

Sam wasn't getting much restful sleep with Lucifer invading his dreams in the guise of Sam's dearly departed Jessica. "When Jessica came back and turned into the Devil and talked to Sam, there was something about that that gave me a chill,"

Above
A confused Castiel tries to explain to the deputy that angels and demons are skirmishing all over the globe.

Above

Dean tries to keep a straight face while Castiel fumbles the role of an FBI agent.

comments associate producer Kristin Cronin. "I think there's just something creepy about doing the Devil stuff." Baer agrees, adding, "Mark Pellegrino's performance as Satan was mesmerizing. What an actor!"

Another actor that stood out in this episode was Misha Collins, who went through a range of dramatic beats from asking Dean for help to visiting a brothel to facing down Archangel Raphael. Producer Jim Michaels thinks Collins' increased presence in season five is a godsend. "I think the introduction of Misha's Castiel as an ally of the boys has added a whole other dynamic range," he states. "Having Castiel in there working with them is another angle for the stories, a nice spoke in the wheel that they haven't had before."

RAPHAEL: Surely you remember Zachariah giving you stomach cancer?
DEAN: Yeah, that was... that was hilarious.
RAPHAEL: Yes, well, he doesn't have anything close to my imagination...

Tobin enjoyed working with Collins, and particularly enjoyed the scene where they trapped Archangel Raphael, played by Demore Barnes, who Tobin characterizes as "a wonderful actor. We played a lot with [where to pitch the] portrayal with him, because he was the first archangel that we met, and archangels are supposed to be more powerful and scarier than our normal angels, so we were playing with: 'How do you make someone scary when they're not really supposed to be that emotional?' It's really just about the amount of power and the threat of control. All very interesting things to explore."

Jared Padalecki loved how this episode turned out, and adds, "We're huge fans of J. Miller Tobin. I look forward to working with him again." ✐

MUSIC

'Simple Man' by Lynyrd Skynyrd
'Devil Sway' by Swank
'Blues Won't Let Me Be' by Left Hand Frank and His Blues Band

Above

Sam is shocked to learn he's destined to be Lucifer's true vessel.

WEEKLY NATIONAL NEWS

Saturday 21 August, 2010

EERIE EQUINE MYSTERY

More details page 26

GASSING UP FOR THE APOCALYPSE

By Jack Walsh

Somebody warn Stephen King — horrors from Hell are loose in his beloved home state of Maine. Better yet, warn everybody! At the very least, stay clear of the Pump 'n' Go on Route 4 in Waterville. Not that there's anything left of it. According to Deputy Walt Farmingham, in the midst of an inexplicable riot of forty people, the gas station was levelled by "an explosion of pure white light — definitely not your usual fireball." He refused to speculate on the record about what really happened out there, but this intrepid reporter overheard FBI Agent Eddie Moscone tell the deputy that it was angels battling demons!

There was only one survivor, mechanic Donnie Finnerman, and he's not talking — he's downright catatonic — but he doesn't have a scratch on him... It's like a miracle from Heaven. TV psychic Jean Edison says the Devil himself is walking the Earth, and has even ventured to suggest that

THE END

Written by:
Ben Edlund

Directed by:
Steve Boyum

Guest Cast: John Paul McGlynn (Gaunt Man), Devyn Dalton (Young Girl), Lexa Doig (Risa), Dwayne Bryshun (Capek), Michael Jonsson (Yager)

Dean is accosted by a preacher outside his hotel in Kansas City but thinks nothing of it. Since Dean is hidden from angel detection by the sigil on his ribs, Castiel finds him by the simple expedient of a phone call. Cass wants to go after the Colt, but Dean insists on sleeping first. He is woken by a call from Sam, who wants to hunt again, but Dean thinks they're weaker together, and refuses to reunite with his brother. He goes back to sleep, only to awaken five years in the future, thanks to Zachariah, who found Dean via the preacher.

The future is a wasteland overrun by people infected with the Croatoan virus. A mob of Crotes spot Dean, but he is rescued by some National Guardsmen. Zachariah warns Dean that this is how the future will be if he says no to being Michael's vessel, then leaves him to stew. Dean goes to Bobby's place, where he finds a bloody, bullet-riddled wheelchair and a picture of Camp Chitaqua. At the camp, he is horrified to find the Impala rotting away, and is then taken prisoner by a future version of himself.

At first Future Dean implies Sam is dead, but after securing the Colt he reveals that Sam said yes to Lucifer, and that Future Dean is going to kill him. He implores Dean to say yes to Michael when he gets back to 2009. Future Dean launches an assault on Lucifer, using his friends — including a practically human hippie Castiel — as decoys. The plan fails miserably, and Dean watches the Devil (in Sam's body) snap Future Dean's neck. Lucifer tells Dean he will always win, but Dean vows to find a way to kill him. Zachariah takes Dean back to the present, but Dean still refuses to be Michael's vessel. Instead, after Castiel rescues him, Dean contacts Sam and tells him they need to stick together and make their own future.

DEAN: Maybe we *are* each other's Achilles heel. Maybe they'll find a way to use us against each other. I don't know. I just know we're all we've got. More than that, we keep each other human.
SAM: Thank you. Really. Thank you. I won't let you down...
DEAN: Oh, I know it. I mean, you are the second best hunter on the planet.

"I thought that 'The End' was a particularly good episode," says executive producer Phil Sgriccia. "Jensen Ackles just hit it out of the park with the performance opposite

his future self."

Ackles was happy with the final result, but he says getting there "was a nightmare. We'd hired an actor to play opposite me and called him 'Diet Jensen' because he was smaller than me, and they put shoulder pads in his jacket, which made his head look too small, like shrunken-head Beetlejuice — poor kid. He immediately was trying to do a performance, and I was like, 'I don't want your performance, because I'm going to do my own and if you start performing I'll react differently than to what I'm going to do.' So I got my stunt double, Todd Scott — who's not an actor, he's never performed, but he knows how to carry himself like Dean — and said, 'You already look like me from behind, so all I need for you to do is read the lines.' He was scared, but he got up there and did it, and it was just as nerve-wracking for him as it was for me.

"For me, as an actor, it was really difficult," continues Ackles. "There were a few days of filming where by the end of the day I was just exhausted; I was mentally bushed. I was doing so much second-guessing of myself as to how I was going to play something on both sides of the camera, then having to remember what I'd done so that I could react to what I'd already filmed. To do that for eight or nine pages a day makes you want to shoot yourself!"

Above

Dean considers taking in a movie, but gets distracted.

Above

Dean is sent to the future by Zachariah and is shocked to discover the Apocalypse has already happened.

In fact, if he had shot himself — Future Dean shooting regular Dean, that is — it would have been believable, seeing as how Future Dean had become somewhat cold-hearted. "I had to be a Dean who was war-torn after five years of affective Apocalypse," notes Ackles. "I had help from our director of photography, Serge Ladouceur. He lit the two Deans differently. He made Future Dean darker and moodier than regular Dean. It's a little thing that probably went unnoticed, but it made it more believable."

ZACHARIAH: The time for tricks is over. Give yourself to Michael. Say "yes," and we can *strike*. Before Lucifer gets to Sam. *Before billions die...*
DEAN: Nah.
ZACHARIAH: *"Nah?"* You telling me you haven't learned your lesson?
DEAN: Oh, I learned a lesson all right... Just not the one you wanted to teach.

Another little thing that added to a scene was the way Chuck acted around Future Dean's enraged lover, Risa. "One of my favorite scenes in 'The End' was the scene with Risa," says director Steve Boyum. "When we rehearsed the scene where Dean runs into her while he's with Chuck, Robert Benedict goes, 'You know, the way I look at this is I've been trying to pick her up this whole time.' So when Chuck goes, 'Hi Risa,' and she just disses him completely, it cracked me up. Robert found that himself, and it was just precious."

Zachariah didn't send Dean to the future to get into love triangles; he wanted to show Dean the future if Dean doesn't say yes to Michael. But was it a real future, or just another one of the angel's tricks? "Yes, it was a real future, and Zachariah saw

MUSIC

'Do You Love Me' by The Contours

it," claims Kurt Fuller. "Just like time is relative, I think he took Dean to a relative future." Executive producer Ben Edlund confirms Fuller's theory. "When the angels took Dean into the future, I believe they went into the future, but the future is a non-constant," he explains. "It could be that this happens or that happens, but it's a self-correcting rough shape. The future can go a number of different ways, and the angels can go into any of these possible futures." In other words, Zachariah chose a possible future to suit his ends. Too bad for him it backfired.

On the other hand, nothing backfired for Boyum. He is thrilled with the way the episode turned out. "'The End' is my favorite *Supernatural* episode that I've done," states Boyum. "It's probably my favorite episode of television that I will ever do. When I saw it, I thought, 'I don't know if I'll ever be able to do another one like this.'"

DEVASTATING DESIGN

Production designer Jerry Wanek reveals how his team created the future for 'The End'. "Just about my whole crew worked with me on *Dark Angel,* where for forty episodes we really got schooled in how to make things look devastated and in a post-apocalyptic state. Wherever we went outside the studio, we had to make it post-apocalyptic. So we knew what read well, what gave us the most mileage. But we could not have done it had we not had our back lot, which was formerly the *Watchmen* set, because you could never do the amount of devastation that we inflicted on those buildings to any downtown area. The city of Vancouver is not going to let you do that. The way Steve Boyum moved the camera through all the stuff that we gave him really maximized it to full effect, so that was also a huge factor in making that work."

DID YOU KNOW?

The crew members that wrecked an Impala for 'The End' "did such a good job of wrecking it that it wasn't recognizable as the Impala," reveals visual effects supervisor Ivan Hayden. So then the visual effects team had to "pretty it up."

FALLEN IDOLS

Written by:
Julie Siege

Directed by:
Jim Conway

Guest Cast: Brad Dryborough (Cal Hopkins), Paul McGillion (Jim Grossman), Daryl Shuttleworth (Sheriff Rick Carnegie), Bruce Harwood (Professor Hill), Jo-Ann Fernandes (Consuela Alvarez), David Livingstone (Abraham Lincoln), Emily Tennant (Ashley), Anja Savcic (Nina), Cynthia Mendez (Cammy), Robert Clarke (Phil Wagner), Paris Hilton (Paris Hilton/Leshi), Paul Statman (Gandhi)

After searching for the Colt for weeks with no leads, Sam and Dean travel to Canton, Ohio, to investigate a man killed in James Dean's cursed car. The car turns out to be a fake, but when another man is murdered by an Abraham Lincoln lookalike, the brothers suspect famous ghosts are killing off their biggest fans. They visit a wax museum with displays that use real artifacts, including Lincoln's stovepipe hat and James Dean's keychain, so the brothers return after hours to burn all the potential ghosts' remains. Then Sam is attacked by Gandhi.

Dean burns wax Gandhi's real bifocals and the ghost disappears, but Sam points out that the ghost didn't scream and burn up, and that Gandhi tried to eat him. When Dean wants to leave, Sam argues that they can't stay together unless Dean starts treating him as a grown-up and trusting his judgement. Then two girls witness their friend being abducted by Paris Hilton, who isn't dead, so the ghost theory is out. Sam examines the first two victims' bodies and discovers they lost more blood than their wounds accounted for. He also finds strange seeds in their stomachs, which indicates they are dealing with the pagan god Leshi, whose forest in the Balkans was cut down for a Yugo car plant.

They return to the museum, where Paris Hilton captures them. The god plans to take on John Winchester's likeness in order to be Dean's hero, but Dean unties himself and attacks her. Leshi Paris whales on Dean until Sam gets free and chops her head off with an iron axe. Before they leave town, Dean admits Sam couldn't have known killing Lilith would start the Apocalypse, and they agree to move forward as equals.

DEAN: Let me get this straight. Your, uh, ultimate hero was not only a short man in diapers, but he was also a *fruitarian?*
SAM: That's not the point.
DEAN: That is good. Even for you, that is good.

"When they first conjured up the episode, the initial reaction in the office was that Paris Hilton probably wouldn't do it," says producer Jim Michaels. "So they started talking about other people, but somebody wisely said, 'Let her say no.' Eric Kripke was very upfront with her that we wanted to make fun of celebrity, and she was game for it. Plus she knew Jared Padalecki [from *House of Wax*], so that might have

had something to do with her decision to participate as well."

"We have some mutual friends from the movie, so it was nice to have her on the show," Padalecki says. "It's funny, people would ask me beforehand, 'What's she like? Is she gonna show up? Is she gonna be drunk?' I was like, 'She's a sweet girl. She'll show up on time, she'll know her lines, and she'll do a great job. And she did. She played exactly the role she was supposed to play. It was fun!" Part of the fun for Padalecki was simulating chopping Paris's head off. "We had a laugh about it," he says. "On the day, I was teasing her about the blood that I was getting on her face from slamming the axe into this gigantic sponge full of fake blood. In *House of Wax* she got a pole through the head, and here I'm chopping her head off. She had a good sense of humor about it all."

"She definitely has a character of herself that she puts on for everybody, but she can turn it off, which was nice to see," says Jensen Ackles. "She was professional. We get people that are actors and they come in and can't do what she did. She was very nice." Stunt coordinator Lou Bollo concurs with Ackles. "You get one version and then you get the real version," Bollo says. "She was always texting and getting her stuff out there to all her fans, but I found her to be really intelligent. I think I had

Above
Sam and Dean rescue a damsel in distress from becoming a snack for the Leshi.

Above

Sam and Dean try to outwit a hungry pagan god.

MUSIC

'Sixteen' by Lucero
'Superstition' by Jeff Beck

about half an hour to give her a little bit of fight training, because she'd never done any on-screen fights in her life, and I found her to be really quick on the uptake. She has a great sense of humor, too. She was just terrific."

"The part where Paris Hilton confronted the boys was on stage," remarks art director John Marcynuk, "but for the rest of the wax museum we went to a location that used to be a library. Actually finding the wax museum items was quite a trial, but we lucked out. We sent one of our set decoration people to a wax museum in Victoria, and they were quite accommodating. They gave us a number of statues that they'd retired, and the writers just wrote to those and it worked out great. That episode was a lot of fun to do."

"The art department is unbelievable," says director Jim Conway. "When we were doing 'Fallen Idols', for the scene where the James Dean car had to be brought to a body shop, we had to clean this real body shop up, and there's this big huge sign on the back wall talking about the prices and all that, and about three hours into shooting I realized that it was our sign. It was aged so beautifully it looked like it

was part of the building, so I was just amazed at how wonderful it was. If you watch TV shows, sometimes the signs give it away in a minute."

Conway also has high praise for the special makeup effects department. "Their makeup stuff is feature quality every week. Nothing scares them — they know exactly how to deliver real good-looking stuff. If you're setting up a scene and it all depends on the guy's head getting cut off and the blood spurting, if it doesn't look good and you have to do it again, it kills your day. So not only do they provide wonderful stuff, but it actually works and does what it's supposed to do."

DEAN: Not a word.
SAM: Dude, you just got *whaled on* by Paris Hilton!
DEAN: Shut up.

One of the things they needed Paris Hilton's severed head to do was roll away from her body. "We pulled a severed head from stock and put a Paris Hilton wig on it," explains Toby Lindala, head of special makeup effects, "and bowled with that on set, just for it to roll a few feet." Then the visual effects department took over and did a CG version of her severed head. "I got to say I killed Paris Hilton — it was *hot!*" jokes visual effects supervisor Ivan Hayden. "We put the gory neck bits and the blood in to flavor it, but we actually had a backup version where we'd rotated the head so you weren't looking up the stump. That's generally what we do — we take it to the extreme and then pull it back. There wasn't a problem with it though, so we were all stoked." ⚡

Above
Dean doesn't want to see Paris Hilton morph into John Winchester.

DID YOU KNOW?
For the stationary car crash scene in the teaser, supervising sound editor Charlie Crutcher says, "We had five seconds to give the sound of James Dean's car going off the cliff, both the swerve and the impact that killed him."

I BELIEVE THE CHILDREN ARE OUR FUTURE

Written by:
Andrew Dabb &
Daniel Loflin

Directed by:
Charles Beeson

Guest Cast: Raquel Riskin (Amber Greer), Andrew Bernard (Jimmy Malloy), Chris Boyd (George Malloy), Patricia Cullen (Francine Malloy), Keith MacKechnie (Jerry), John F. Parker (Mr. Stanley), Patrick Keating (Oscar), Christopher Delisle (Troy Stokes), Dalila Bela (Agnes Stokes), Mark Acheson (Tooth Fairy), Neelam Khabra (Hot Nurse Jen Fremont), Joe-Norman Shaw (Mailman), Gattlin Griffith (Jesse Turner), Ever Carradine (Julia Wright)

In Alliance, Nebraska, itching powder causes a teenage girl to claw her brains out, and a joy buzzer electrocutes a man to death. The joy buzzer doesn't even have batteries, yet Dean cooks an entire ham with it. Sam and Dean assume the objects are cursed and confront the man who sold them, but he turns out to be innocent. Next, a big, bearded Tooth Fairy yanks out a man's teeth, two boys are hospitalized with stomach ulcers from mixing Pop Rocks and Coke, and another boy's face freezes when he makes a horrible expression.

It turns out that an eleven-year-old named Jesse is unknowingly making everything he believes come true. The boy was adopted, so the Winchesters visit his biological mother, who was possessed and impregnated by a demon, but got control of her body just after giving birth and forced the demon out. Castiel informs Sam and Dean that the child is an anti-Christ, powerful enough to destroy angels with a word. Sam thinks Jesse will choose the side of good if given the chance, but Castiel feels Jesse must be eliminated.

When Cass tries to kill Jesse, the anti-Christ turns the angel into a small toy. Sam and Dean try to get Jesse to go with them to Bobby's for superhero training, but the demon that sired him arrives in his biological mother's body. She tells Jesse everyone lied to him, but Sam convinces him he doesn't have to be a monster. Jesse exorcises the demon from his mother, puts everyone back to normal, then takes his adoptive parents and vanishes. Castiel says Jesse can't be found unless he wants to be, which is fine with the boys, so long as Lucifer can't find him either.

SAM: **He wrote up a description: five-foot-ten, 350 pounds, wings, and a pink tutu. Said it was the Tooth Fairy.**
DEAN: **So he's obviously whacked out on painkillers.**
SAM: **Maybe. Whatever it was got past locked doors and windows without triggering the alarm.**
DEAN: **Come on, *Tooth Fairy?***
SAM: **And they left thirty-two quarters underneath his pillow. One for each tooth.**

The writing team comprised of story editors Andrew Dabb and Daniel Loflin seem to enjoy messing with Jensen Ackles. In 'Yellow Fever' they made him scream like a

Above

Sam and Dean
ask Jesse (Gattlin
Griffith) the anti-
Christ to confirm the
identity of the Tooth
Fairy.

girl, in 'After School Special' they put him in plum-smuggler shorts, and in 'I Believe the Children Are Our Future' they made him eat tons of ham, not to mention the hairy hand incident. It makes one wonder if he has threatened to inflict bodily harm on the writers if they persist in this manner. "He punched me!" Dabb says jokingly. "No, he didn't. I think he enjoys being goofy every once in a while. In season six, we're going to send him to a renaissance fair. No, just kidding." Maybe.

"The ham!" exclaims property master Chris Cooper in mock horror. "What an event that was. Whatever we do, we have to have multiples, and when you're cutting pieces off of a ham, getting the cut multiples to look the same is a huge challenge. On top of that it was a funny situation because you don't just cook a pork shoulder and get a ham. The pork has to be cured, and there are several ways of curing it, which makes it change color, and blah, blah, blah."

Dabb bought a joy buzzer for the office, but it didn't make magic ham. "Nobody else besides he and I played with it," states Loflin, "but production assistant Jenny Klein gave us whoopee cushions for Christmas." The writers haven't had the nerve to use the cushions on their bosses yet, but Dabb says, "I think first thing next season, Bob Singer's in for a surprise." Loflin adds, "I would absolutely use it on Eric Kripke. He would have a great sense of humor about it. But it'd be difficult to get

Above

Castiel believes he must kill the anti-Christ.

DID YOU KNOW?

When on the trail of their father in the Pilot, Sam and Dean discover John Winchester's recently vacated motel room, where he had left his research plastered on the walls. One of the items is an article entitled "My Son the Cambion." Cambion is another name for the anti-Christ.

it where he didn't see it. If he was in the middle of saying something, he sat down without looking, and the actual whoopee cushion performed as it's designed to, no question that would be *hilarious*, but these things never work out. So Castiel with the whoopee cushion and how extended it was? That would never happen like that in reality. That's total TV."

DEAN: You know, I'm starting to get why parents lie to their kids. You know, you want them to believe that the worst thing out there is mixing Pop Rocks and Coke; protect them from the real evil. You want them going to bed feeling safe. If that means lying to them, so be it. The more I think about it, the more I wish Dad had lied to us.
SAM: Yeah, me too.

That sequence almost didn't happen at all, though. "At first, Jensen, Jared, and I all resisted it," states Misha Collins. "We called Eric on the phone and were like, 'The whoopee cushion is stupid.' We each had a turn on the phone trying to convince him to take the whoopee cushion out of the scene. We were like, 'We're here rehearsing and it's just not funny. It's screwing up the scene.' He insisted it was going to work, and then when we started shooting the scene we couldn't stop laughing! It took forever to shoot because first we were being obstinate, annoying actors and we wouldn't start shooting it, and then once we did start, we couldn't actually do it because we were laughing too hard."

Another thing that made them laugh was playing with the Castiel action figure. Ackles claims he did some fun things with the mini-Misha, "But I'd probably get in trouble if I told you," he teases, "so we'll just leave that one to the imagination." Collins likewise wouldn't confirm or deny any plans on his part for absconding with one of the action figures. "I thought they would've given me one of them," Collins says. "There's a point of contention here between me and the props department." Perhaps with director Charles Beeson, as well, since he made sure no one pocketed one of the unique toys. "Everyone tried to sneak off with them," Beeson says. "We had to have body searches every day to make sure the Castiel action figures never left the set."

For his part, Cooper really enjoyed creating the toys. "We used a very talented local sculptor," he reveals. "The small knife was awesome, and getting the trench coat right was a big part of making that action figure look cool."

Costume designer Diane Widas knows all about using coats and other articles of clothing to make characters look cool, or uncool. In this episode, she particularly loved working on the Tooth Fairy's costume. "Just doing the research for the Tooth Fairy and seeing how many bizarre male tooth fairies are out there and then extrapolating and making our own version of it was really fun. That was definitely a highlight of season five."

Widas almost missed out on the opportunity because an auditioning actor had his own costume. According to Beeson, "When we were casting, this huge guy turned up in the full costume — pink leotard, a tutu and shoes, a wand and a crown, everything. I looked at him, and with a straight face I asked, 'What part did you come for?' He laughed and then told me that he'd come like that on the bus. He didn't get the part, so god knows what happened to him." ✐

A Closer Look At:
FOREST GODS

Leshi is a pagan god who watched over a forest in the Balkans. So infamous was she in her heyday that her name spread across Eastern Europe and all manner of wood spirits, forest gods, and woodland shapeshifters were soon called by similar names, such as Leshy, Leszi, Lesovy, and Lesovik.

Forest gods can take on the form of *anything* they touch, from humans to wolves, bears, trees, even mushrooms, but they prefer forms that inspire idolatry, since they draw their strength from consuming the blood of their most ardent worshippers. They fill their victims' stomachs with seeds, presumably so that the decomposing corpses will provide ready-made fertilizer to feed the seeds and guarantee the replenishment of the forest.

That's not to say that non-worshippers are safe. Far from it. These creatures can read minds. They will ascertain who you admire most, then take on that form. They need something that person has touched, though, so if you still have that sweat-stained towel your favorite rock star threw into the audience, you should consider washing it (or burning it).

DEAN: So you're saying we've got two super-famous, super-pissed-off ghosts killing their... super-fans?
SAM: That's what it looks like.

Even if a forest god can't get its hands on anything your idol has touched, that doesn't mean you're free to traverse their territory. They don't like trespassers, and they amuse themselves by getting people lost in the woods. They will take on the form of a distinctive tree and continually move into your path to make you think you're going in circles, bewildering your sense of direction. They will erase your footprints, trick you into eating poisonous mushrooms, and take on the form of vicious animals to chase and terrify you. Strangely, they also enjoy tickling people to death.

There is a rumor these forest gods can be defeated by putting your shoes on the wrong feet and your clothes on backward, which confuses them about which way you're going and, frustrated, they will leave you alone. By all other indications, though, they are quite clever, so odds are this is just a cruel joke perpetrated by locals in hopes that the gods will eat their fill of outsiders.

Nonetheless, there are those who willingly sacrifice themselves. When properly appeased, these forest masters protect hunters and herdsmen in the forest, ensure good crops for the local farmers, and give their most favored worshippers magical powers.

So beware of mischievous, bloodthirsty shapeshifters in the forests, or wax museums, or anywhere nowadays, and keep an iron axe handy. Just don't accidentally decapitate your *real* idols.

A Closer Look At:
DEMON SPAWN

When most Christians think of an anti-Christ, they think of a wolf in sheep's clothing — or, rather, a devil in sheep's clothing, seeing as how the anti-Christ is believed to be the Devil's son, and Christ is also known as the Lamb of God. The common interpretation of the biblical references is that the anti-Christ is an End Times leader who deceives people into thinking he will provide salvation from the Apocalypse, but instead leads his followers to their damnation.

"We wanted to present the anti-Christ in a slightly different way," states story editor Andrew Dabb. "The anti-Christ in the Bible is really less of a fighter and more of a talker. So we looked at the anti-Christ more as a literal definition. Christ was born of a virgin human woman, but was divine, and our anti-Christ is born of a virgin human woman, but is demonic."

Supernatural's anti-Christ isn't Lucifer's child, he is simply demon spawn, which extends the mythology beyond Christianity to other cultures where human-demon hybrids are known by names such as cambion and katako.

Of course, one could argue that Sam Winchester is demonic as well, yet he always tries to do the right thing and fights on the side of good, so you shouldn't assume that having demon blood inside him makes anti-Christ Jesse Turner evil.

SAM: Okay, so whatever's doing this is reshaping reality. It has the powers of a god, or a Trickster.
DEAN: And the sense of humor of a nine-year-old.
SAM: Or you.

What isn't known for sure is exactly how they are conceived. The popular theory is that a succubus has sex with a human male, steals his seed, and transfers the human seed to an incubus, who then uses the demon-tainted seed to impregnate a human woman. In the case of Jesse Turner, his mother wasn't even aware she had been raped by an incubus, perhaps because she was already possessed by the demon that stayed with her throughout the pregnancy.

Fortunately, it doesn't happen often. Even a single demon spawn is dangerous enough, believed to be one of the Devil's greatest weapons in the war against Heaven. The anti-Christ's powers include changing his thoughts to reality, manifesting his anger as a destructive force, exorcising demons, teleportation, and the ability to hide from demons and angels.

The angel Castiel fears that Jesse could destroy all the angels as easily as turning one into a toy, but so long as the child stays hidden and is raised by good parents, that will hopefully never happen.

THE CURIOUS CASE OF DEAN WINCHESTER

Teleplay by:
Sera Gamble

Story by:
Sera Gamble
& Jenny Klein

Directed by:
Robert Singer

Guest Cast: Pascale Hutton (Lia), Daniel Arnold (Xavier), Monica Mustelier (Bridget), Veena Sood (Dr. Aldrich), Elan Ross Gibson (Mona Whitlow), Christopher Russell (Cliff Whitlow), Matthew Robert Kelly (Bartender), Rob Heschl (Craig), Daesha Danielle Usman (Maid), Robert Hewko (Hesh), Hal Ozsan (Patrick), Chad Everett (Old Dean)

After a twenty-five-year-old man dies of old age, the Winchesters look for similar cases and find the opposite: a man in his sixties, reported missing, turns up in a motel with two hookers, sporting a twenty-two-year-old body. When they threaten to tell his wife, the man reveals he won years of his life in a poker game. He describes a "miracle worker" named Patrick, but says Patrick moves around a lot, so Sam and Dean split up to scour the local bars.

In one of the bars, Dean runs into Bobby, who has just played Patrick and lost twenty-five years (making Bobby twenty-five years older), so Dean accosts Patrick at gunpoint and demands he restore Bobby's years. But Patrick is a powerful nine hundred-year-old witch, and is unphased, saying a bullet would just "tickle" him. He tells Dean he will have to play him for the years. Patrick gives Dean fifty chips for the poker game, twenty-five of which Dean immediately cashes in for Bobby. Dean loses the game, and his remaining twenty-five chips/years, making him eighty years old! Then Sam and Dean try to steal poker chips from Patrick's apartment, but they are caught and the witch gives Sam gonorrhea.

Bobby wants to play again, as he believes he is useless confined to his wheelchair, so he's willing to risk killing himself, but the brothers won't hear of it. Shockingly, Patrick's immortal girlfriend, Lia, gives them a spell that will reverse all of Patrick's magic. Sam gets into a poker game with Patrick in order to get a DNA-laden toothpick to Bobby in order to cast the spell, but it doesn't work because Patrick tricked Sam with a clean toothpick. Now angry, Patrick gives Dean a heart attack, but Sam wins the poker game, saving Dean. Afterward, Lia plays Patrick and purposely loses, since she's no longer able to cope with having outlived her daughter and all those she loves. Meanwhile, Dean makes Bobby promise not to commit suicide.

DEAN: You don't stop being a soldier 'cause you got wounded in battle. Okay? No matter *what* shape you're in, bottom line is you're *family*. I don't know if you've noticed, but me and Sam, we don't have much left. I can't do this without you. I can't. So don't you dare think about checking out. I don't wanna hear that again.
BOBBY: Okay.
DEAN: Okay. Good.
BOBBY: Thanks. Now are we done feeling our feelings? Because I'd like to get out of this room before we both start growing lady parts.

Bobby has been a father figure to Sam and Dean pretty much since the day their actual father disappeared, and while older than John Winchester, Bobby has always been a vibrant hunter, so to see him aged by twenty-five years in 'The Curious Case of Dean Winchester' is quite the contrast to what we're used to seeing. Nonetheless, Toby Lindala, head of special makeup effects, says the aging they did on Jim Beaver "was just subtle stuff — Jim didn't like it being called 'subtle', though — but it was just latex and paint on him. We did a couple of subtle tricks where we did little tabs to adjust the shape of his outer eyes, give more weight to the lids. I'm really happy with the way that came across, and he was great to work with."

Beaver would have gladly let them make him look fifty years older if they'd wanted to. "I was just happy to get out of the house," he says, seeing as how this was Bobby's first outing since leaving the hospital in a wheelchair. He didn't have any action scenes in this episode, but that's fine by Beaver. He enjoyed the scenes where he discussed his suicidal tendencies and where Dean made him promise not to follow through on his death wish. "For me, what's most fun is what's most dramatic," Beaver says. "While it's a lot of fun to do the special effects and the fights and stuff, where I really enjoy it is just a couple of actors playing a scene together, playing a meaningful conversation together. The heart of any good show, no matter how great the special effects and the technical wizardry are, is the emotion between the characters. That was a place where we really got to play straight up emotion; people say what's on

Above
Witch Patrick (Hal Ozsan) contemplates his next move.

Above

Bobby tries not to have a heart attack while Dean buys into a magical poker game.

Opposite

Dean listens to what Bobby has to say.

their mind and in their hearts, and reveal what's in their hearts, without covering it up, without being glib. There's an awful lot of glibness in this show. I mean, the boys in particular are smartasses. It doesn't have to be Shakespeare; it can be some kiddy show if you find those moments to play. They're always, at least for me, the most rewarding, and this show is rich with stuff like that."

BOBBY: Can you straighten up?
OLD DEAN: Yeah, but a little sympathy wouldn't hurt.
BOBBY: Butt cheek tingling?
OLD DEAN: Well, that's kinda personal—
BOBBY: So, yeah? It's *sciatica*. You'll live. Keep digging.
OLD DEAN: You know, Bobby, killing you is officially on my Bucket List.

Although it was suicidal for Bobby to risk twenty-five years of his life, you can't blame him for hoping that if he won, along with becoming twenty-five years younger, he would also be healing his legs. However, according to executive producer Sera Gamble, there was never any chance that Bobby would walk out of this episode on healthy young legs. "No, we only ever had the idea of having him lose as a way into telling a story about Dean being super-old," she says.

It would have taken too long in the prosthetics chair to make Jensen Ackles look super-old, but with Ackles' father being an actor, too, it would have been interesting

DID YOU KNOW?

The Golden Palace motel that Cliff Whitlow frequented was called Whisper Lane Motel in the teleplay.

to see him tackle the role. "He didn't seem to mind [not getting offered the part]," Ackles says, the reason being that his father is not fifty years older than him. "Chad Everett did an awesome job," Ackles points out. "I told Chad, 'Look, man, if I look like you when I'm your age, I'll be one happy son-of-a-bitch.' He actually came on set a few days before and just watched me work — studied my mannerisms and the things that I would do as Dean. He watched some of the episodes, too, but he wanted to see how I was doing it in person and I think it really helped him. I was astonished at his performance and what he did."

Production assistant Jenny Klein loved Chad Everett's performance. "He does an

excellent Dean Winchester," she enthused. Klein pitched the initial idea behind this story, which she says, "Eric and Sera made into something even better. I got a shared story credit on it with Sera, and I feel really lucky. It was really cool to finally see it on TV. Plus, it was really fun to see when Old Dean turns back into regular Dean and Jensen did that little jump."

Composer Christopher Lennertz had fun with this episode as well. "I played comedy more than usual in this episode. Most of the time we still have a classic rock bit through the comedy, but because Dean got old we decided to go a little more jazz. Like when Dean was trying to get up all those flights of steps and was totally winded, we thought it'd be funny to have a lumbering trombone solo. That will never happen again, but for this it really worked out well."

Executive producer Robert Singer directed 'The Curious Case of Dean Winchester' and is known to be a poker player, but if given the opportunity to play for years of his life, he would pass. "No," he says, "that's risking too much." ✐

CHANGING CHANNELS

Written by:
Jeremy Carver

Directed by:
Charles Beeson

Guest Cast: Richard Speight Jr. (The Trickster/Gabriel), Steve Bacic (Dr. Sexy), Christine Chatelain (Dr. Piccolo), William MacDonald (Sheriff Cliff Smalls), Sarah Jane Redmond (Kathy Randolph), Sarah Smyth (Intern), Beatrice Ilg (Girl In Bikini), Bart Anderson (Mr. Beale), Chasty Ballesteros (Nurse), Hiro Kanagawa (Game Show Host), Marcia Yu (Game Show Girl), Marita Eason (Yoga Woman), Ken Camroux-Taylor (Sofa Man), Garnet Harding (CSI Tech), Gabriel Carter (Beat Cop)

When a man in Wellington, Ohio, has his head ripped off by the Incredible Hulk, Sam and Dean realize they're dealing with the Trickster. The Trickster traps them in TV land, starting with *Dr. Sexy, M.D.* He tells them they have to play their parts, which means Sam has to act like a doctor to save Dean when he's shot. Then in a Japanese game show, Dean speaks Japanese just by believing he can, thereby saving himself from the "nut-cracker." Castiel suddenly arrives and tries to free the brothers, but is quickly zapped away by the Trickster.

After a herpes commercial, the brothers are put into a sitcom, where Castiel returns. The angel warns them that the Trickster is stronger than he should be, but the Trickster zaps Castiel away again. The Trickster tells the boys to play their roles in real life and say yes to Michael and Lucifer, or else stay in TV land forever. Sam and Dean then find themselves in a procedural cop show, where they seemingly manage to kill the Trickster, but the next morning, Sam awakes and finds he has become a talking version of the Impala.

Dean calls out to the Trickster, claiming he and Sam are ready to say yes, but it's a ruse and he traps the Trickster in a ring of Holy Fire. TV land vanishes and the Trickster admits to being Gabriel, one of the archangels. Unable to bear watching his father and brothers fight, Gabriel ran away from Heaven and disguised himself as Loki, the Trickster. He describes the similarities between Sam and Dean and Lucifer and Michael, and claims the Winchesters are destined to be the vessels, and that one brother has to kill the other. To break the stalemate, Gabriel brings Castiel back, then Dean frees Gabriel, and they go their separate ways.

TRICKSTER: I *am* the Trickster.
DEAN: Or maybe you're not. Maybe you've always been an angel.
TRICKSTER: A *what*? Somebody slip a mickey in your power shake, kid?
DEAN: I'll tell you what, you just jump out of the Holy Fire, and we'll call it our mistake.

"The clear winner for my favorite episode of *Supernatural*, period, is 'Changing Channels'," states creator Eric Kripke. "Of anything we've ever done on *Supernatural*, it's the closest approximation of my true sense of humor, which is to say, *juvenile*. I

just loved it. On top of that, to have it not just be an exercise in whimsy, but have a solid and unexpected mythology reason for it, really grounded it.

"The idea originated with Jeremy Carver," Kripke continues. "He began by saying, 'This pitch is stupid and you're not gonna wanna do it, but I'm just going to say it so that I can get it out of the way. I wanna do *Supernatural* as a half-hour sitcom. We'd have the laugh track and a whacky neighbor and two goofy monster-hunting brothers who live in a motel and all the wackiness and adventures they have.' My initial reaction was, 'I love it! We have to do it. But they can't live in a sitcom for the whole episode, so let's figure out other TV genres we wanna have fun with.' We knew we wanted to parody *CSI* and *Grey's Anatomy*, because they were our timeslot competition. They're such monster hits, so I always say we're the Japanese businessman cowering for cover beneath Godzilla and Mothra. We're just trying to dodge debris. So it felt right to take out a slingshot and take a few shots at those shows.

"Then Ben Edlund said, 'We really should do a herpes commercial and build it into the show as if it's a real commercial.' We became enamored of that idea, but the network said, 'We want to make sure everyone knows that's still part of the show and they don't change the channel or fast-forward on their TiVos or whatever.' We said, 'But that's the entire point — it rewards people that are paying attention.' The network got really nervous, but we stubbornly insisted on doing what we were gonna do.

"Then we were talking about the shows we loved as kids in which the cars were characters, so we thought, 'We should do *Knight Rider*, except that Sam is the car.'

Above

Dr. Sexy is revealed

to be the Winchester

brothers' classic

adversary, the

Trickster (Richard

Speight Jr.).

Opposite

The Trickster is

revealed to be the

archangel Gabriel.

We were like, 'How much crazier can this episode get?' but it always found a way to get one notch crazier. I think the Japanese game show just came out of a desire to watch the guys get hit in the balls. Purely juvenile."

"I was so happy during the nut-cracker scene," says Jensen Ackles with a laugh, "because generally Dean gets the brunt of all the physical practical jokes, and it was nice to actually have Sam get it." In fact, when they filmed the game show, Jared Padalecki was "extremely nervous. I was standing in those ski boots with that big metal bar there, and Lou Bollo showed me how far it would go — but I still put a cup on! I grew up playing football, so I've been hit there before with a cup. It doesn't feel good, but it doesn't make you throw up like getting hit without it. I was definitely nervous, but it was pretty funny."

"When we did the game show I was crying with laughter the whole time," concurs director Charles Beeson. "We got the crew to do the laughter and the 'oohs' and 'ahhs', which gave the whole thing life." Editor Tom McQuade would have loved to be in the audience for that, saying, "I hope nut-cracker goes down in TV history!

"That whole episode was a hoot to cut," adds McQuade. "Tears were rolling from my eyes from laughing." Composer Jay Gruska also found the whole episode "hysterical. Writing that theme song as if it was a 1980s sitcom theme was an incredible amount of fun," he says. "You gotta love the sitcom!" exclaims Richard Speight Jr. "How many times have we watched terrible sitcoms on TV and thought,

'Who's laughing at this? Who did they put in the audience?'

"I had some friends who'd never seen the show, so I told them to check it out," Speight continues. "Well, 'Changing Channels' opens with a really weird, goofy spoof of sitcoms, so my friends found it completely confusing!"

TRICKSTER: So, boys, now what? Stare at each other for the rest of eternity?
DEAN: Well, first of all you're gonna bring Cass back from wherever you stashed him.
TRICKSTER: Oh, am I?
DEAN: Yeah. Or we're going to dunk you in some holy oil, and deep-fry ourselves an archangel.

Then again, it could have been even more confusing. Who knows what else went through the writers' minds? "We kicked around a number of things," says executive producer Robert Singer, "but we didn't want to overdo it and make it such a joke that there wouldn't really be room to tell a story in there. There were plenty of other things we could've mocked. Imagine if the show had opened on a spoof of Emeril Lagasse banishing angels with Enochian sigils drawn in pork blood, shouting his trademark, "Bam!"

"You get to do things on this show that you'll remember for a long time," Singer concludes. "'Changing Channels' was one of them." ✍

MUSIC

'Move You'
by Anya Marina
'Not a Through Street'
by Anya Marina
'The Knight Rider
Theme' by Stu Phillips
'Something Real'
by Renee Stahl
'I Love to See You
Happy (Livin' My Life)'
by Robbi Spencer

THE REAL GHOSTBUSTERS

Teleplay by:
Eric Kripke

Story by:
Nancy Weiner

Directed by:
Jim Conway

Guest Cast: Emily Perkins (Becky Rosen), Crystal Lowe (Fake Leticia Gore), Teagan Rae Avoledo (Real Leticia Gore), Kayla Doerksen (Maid), John Shaw (Real Hotel Manager), Scott Patey (Fanboy), Amitai Marmorstein (Friend), Darien Provost (Scalped Boy), Connor Stanhope (Little Boy #1), Connor Beardmore (Little Boy #2), Luke Gair (Little Boy #3), Jonathan Bruce (Rollie), Ken Lawson (Hookman), Paul Andrich (Scarecrow), Devin Ratray (Demian), Ernie Grunwald (Barnes)

A "life or death" text message from Chuck brings Sam and Dean to the Pineview Hotel, but it was just a ruse by number-one-fan Becky to get them to the first ever *Supernatural* convention. Everywhere they turn there's someone acting like Sam or Dean or other *Supernatural* characters, such as the Hook Man, the scarecrow, Bobby, and Ash. A screaming maid gets the brothers' attention until they realize she's a character in a live action role playing game. But the game is based on a real ghost story, and the real ghosts soon reveal themselves.

While several fake Winchesters dressed as FBI agents talk to a fake hotel manager, the real Winchesters talk to the real manager, who admits the hotel is haunted by Leticia Gore, who ran the orphanage that was turned into the hotel and apparently killed four boys, then herself. Two convention attendees, Barnes and Demian, larping as Sam and Dean, accompany the boys to the adjoining cemetery, but freak out when they realize Dean is digging up a real corpse. Then they nearly have their hearts ripped out by Gore's ghost before Dean burns the bones.

Back at the hotel, they encounter Gore's ghostly son, who had been scalped. He tells the brothers that the other boys killed him, and that his mother's ghost kept the naughty boys' ghosts from killing everyone. The spirits then lock everyone inside the hotel, but an actress dressed like Gore distracts them long enough for Demian and Barnes to slip out. The ghosts come close to scalping Sam and Dean, but the Winchester wannabes burn the children's bones. Later, Becky shares information she found in Chuck's books — Bela gave the Colt to Lilith's right-hand man (and Crossroads Demon), Crowley. So the brothers set off on a demon hunt.

DEMIAN: No offence, but I'm not sure you get what the story's about.
DEAN: That so?
DEMIAN: Alright, look, in real life, he sells stereo equipment, I fix copiers. *Our* lives suck. But to be Sam and Dean — to wake up every morning and save the world, to have a brother who would *die* for you... Well, who *wouldn't* want that?
DEAN: Maybe you've got a point.

"While we were in the middle of shooting 'The Monster at the End of This Book', Nancy Weiner, the writers' assistant, said to me, 'You know, if people really do larp, wouldn't they larp as Sam and Dean? Then one day Sam and Dean could go to a

Supernatural convention where everyone's dressed as Sam and Dean.' I said, 'That's terrific. We're adding that to the board,' and sure enough, we did it in season five," shares creator Eric Kripke. "The notion of the real characters intermingling with all these people who are dressed as them and believe them to be fictional was a concept that we really wanted to execute because we felt it'd lead to all sorts of funny and quirky moments."

Costume designer Diane Widas says "it was totally fun" dressing the larping Sams and Deans. "First off was figuring out the most iconic look of the boys so that the audience would know what we were doing. The leather jacket for Dean is obviously the biggest thing. It's sort of a seventies style, so we went through every vintage shop in Vancouver. It worked out really well, and everybody got into it on set." Along with the fake costumes, they needed fake props. "We prepped that episode just as the Halloween stuff was coming out, so it was like a gift from the heavens," states property master Chris Cooper. "We even found toy sawed-off shotguns."

Another part of the episode that was not too far from reality was the question and answer session with Chuck. "That was a little exaggerated because we were going for comedy," notes Kripke, "but the way certain people really try to punish you with their questions, how they're really aggressive in terms of pointing out the flaws of the show, that part can sometimes be painfully accurate."

"One of the weirder things to have happened to me in terms of life versus art

Above
Chuck slowly but surely overcomes his stage fright.

DID YOU KNOW?
Emily Perkins costarred in the *Ginger Snaps* trilogy of horror films with Katharine Isabelle, who played Ava Wilson, one of the psychic children, in season two's 'Hunted' and 'All Hell Breaks Loose, Part One'.

Above

Dean and Sam discuss how it was a mistake to banish Leticia Gore's ghost.

MUSIC

'Topsy Turvy' by The Bughouse Five
'Whiskey' by Swank
'Ain't Got Nobody' by Hound Dog Taylor
'Ring-A-Ling' by Miss Eighty 6
'Trouble Baby' by The Bughouse Five

was when literally two nights after 'The Real Ghostbusters' aired I was at my first *Supernatural* convention," says Rob Benedict, "and the very first thing I did was walk out on a stage and take questions. I was like, 'What? Where? Oh my god, is this real? Who am I?' I kind of imitated my character, shaking with the bottle of water, and everybody laughed, so I thought, 'Okay, this is kind of cool.' It was the friendliest audience, so after that it was good. Everybody who went to the actual convention was not nearly as scary as the fans at the TV convention, and not as many people dressed up in costumes."

Were there any super-fans like Becky Rosen, though? "Becky is totally cute, but geeky," says Widas. "She's somebody that Chuck would be attracted to. For the conference we made her a quirky sexy; her style is a little off the beaten path." Unfortunately for Becky, Sam didn't notice her sex appeal, even when she licked her hand and blew him a kiss. "That was in the script," says Emily Perkins, "but they had me try a bunch of different things. They were like, 'Okay, try rubbing your chest,' and 'Try licking your hand slowly and sucking on your fingers.' I had quite a blush after I finished filming that!"

Another moment that left Perkins blushing came when she was standing next to Jared and Jensen while the cameraman was lining up a shot. "We were at the back of the convention room and there were all these chairs, and the cameraman said, 'Oh, Emily, I'm trying to line up some shots, can you stand up please?' I was like, 'I *am* standing.' I'm so much shorter than them that it looked like I was sitting down. It

was a little embarrassing, but everyone got a good laugh out of that."

Despite appearances, the convention was not filmed at an actual hotel. "That was the Stanley Park Pavilion," explains locations manager Russ Hamilton. "It was difficult for us to find a hotel we could shoot at, one that we could afford to rent for over a week and dress it so it could service the story."

BECKY: Chuck and I, we found each other. My Yin to his proud Yang. And, well, the heart wants what the heart wants. I'm so, so sorry.
CHUCK: Yeah, Sam. You know — *sorry.*
BECKY: Will you be alright?
SAM: Honestly, I don't know. I'll just have to find a way to keep living, I guess.

The part of the story that surprised Perkins was that Becky ended up with Chuck, but she says, "That was very cute. He has his little hero moment and she gets turned on by that." In fact, Perkins would like to see Becky have her own hero moment. "I think that getting in on the hunting with the Winchesters would be a total dream come true for Becky. She would be orgasmic!"

"Emily Perkins is a Vancouver girl, and she's fantastically funny, just perfect for the character," comments director Jim Conway, "and Rob Benedict's one of the funniest guys I've ever seen. The whole episode was well cast and a lot of fun to do. 'The Real Ghostbusters' is my favorite of the ones I've directed because it was a perfect blend of comedy and horror." ✐

ABANDON ALL HOPE

Written by:
Ben Edlund

Directed by:
Phil Sgriccia

Guest Cast: Samantha Ferris (Ellen Harvelle), Alona Tal (Jo Harvelle), Rachel Miner (Meg), L. Harvey Gold (Mr. Pendleton), Darryl Scheelar (Guard #1), Louis Paquette (Guard #2), Dawn Chubai (Newscaster)

C astiel locates Crowley's mansion, but the angel can't enter due to Enochian warding magic. With Jo Harvelle's help, Sam and Dean sneak in, but Crowley was expecting the brothers. Then the demon unexpectedly hands the Colt over to Sam. He *wants* the Winchesters to kill Lucifer, because he believes that after the humans are wiped out, the demons will be next. He even tells them where to find the Devil. The Winchesters, the Harvelles, Castiel, and Bobby then gather at Bobby's place for what they believe might be their last night on Earth, where they drink and take a group photo.

Everyone except Bobby heads for Carthage, Missouri. Once there, Castiel spots Reapers everywhere. When he investigates he is trapped in a ring of Holy Fire by Lucifer. Meg arrives and looses hellhounds on the others. While saving Dean from one of the beasts, Jo is wounded by another. They take shelter in a hardware store, and Dean calls Bobby, who informs him that Lucifer is summoning the Horseman Death. Jo knows she's not going to make it, so she suggests they build a bomb. Ellen insists on staying with her daughter. Dean kisses Jo goodbye, then he and Sam sneak away. Jo dies in her mother's arms, then Ellen lets the hellhounds in and blows up the building.

Sam distracts Lucifer while Dean sneaks up and shoots the Devil in the head. At first it seems to have worked, but Lucifer recovers. Meanwhile, Castiel knocks Meg onto the Holy Fire and climbs over her to get free. With Lucifer busy sacrificing demon-possessed townsfolk to Death, Castiel teleports the Winchesters back to Bobby's. A devastated Bobby tosses their group photo onto the fire, and he and the brothers mourn the loss of their friends.

CROWLEY: I want you to take *this thing* to Lucifer and empty it into his face.
DEAN: Uh-huh. Okay. And why exactly would *you* want the Devil dead?
CROWLEY: It's called *survival*. But I forgot, you two at best are *functional morons*.
DEAN: Yeah? You're functioning — morons.

"I think 'Abandon All Hope' is the best episode Phil Sgriccia's ever directed, and he's done a lot of really great ones," points out executive producer Sera Gamble. "The scene in the building with Jo and Ellen was so emotional, and it highlighted the cost

Above
Sam and Dean have
a hard time trusting
Crowley.

of the Apocalypse in this personal way that I thought was very effective. It's the only time I've ever watched the show and actually welled up. Tears were shed! I went to Eric Kripke and said, 'The director's cut of 510 just made me cry — real tears were rolling down my cheeks,' and he was like, 'Me too!'"

In fact, creator Eric Kripke says, "When Ben Edlund submitted the script, I read it and I started crying. I've never cried before or after from anything on *Supernatural*. It was the way he staged it, with Jo dying in Ellen's arms. What we'd talked about in the outline was that both of them were scared and pushing a button and did a very *Thelma & Louise* thing, blowing up the store together. One of the reasons their death scene is so wonderful is I think they were saying, 'We're going to make you miss us, you sons-of-bitches' — talking to me and Ben. Samantha and Alona gave such an unbelievable performance that everyone who watched the film in the editing room was crying. We were all doing that thing where you rub your eye and say, 'Oh, I've got something in my eye.'"

Before the film made its way to post-production, the crew in Vancouver had shed some tears during the filming of the scene. "It was tough because everyone really

Above

Lucifer traps Castiel in a ring of Holy Fire.

likes Samantha and Alona, and they were very sad to see those characters go," says executive producer Phil Sgriccia. "We did a little video tribute to them. Kristin Cronin, our associate producer, put together footage of Alona and Samantha set to Tom Jones' 'She's a Lady'. We gave them copies of that, so it was fun and sad." Alona Tal was very moved by the DVD. "That was amazing, because both Sam and I have been recurring in guest spots on different shows, and none of them have ever done that," she says. "It said, 'To Sam and Alona. Thanks for everything,'" Samantha Ferris reveals. "It made me bawl my eyes out."

Tal did get a good laugh out of the scene leading up to her death, however. "Filming the scene where you see the hellhounds coming up to me and knocking me down was one of the funniest experiences," she says, "because in order to indicate when it was time to get hit or turn around, the camera guy *woofed*. That was hysterical. I enjoyed having to shoot the gun too; that was a trip for me."

Ferris, on the other hand, didn't have a fun experience with her gun. "I've handled a lot of guns on the show," Ferris says, "but not live ammunition, and you have to be very respectful of live ammunition. Even though they're blanks, you never point a gun toward anybody. I kept having problems cocking the gun. I'd take two shots — *bang, bang* — then go to cock it and it'd jam. About the fourth time it happened, I turn around, I've got the gun in my hand and I'm flagging it around at the boys and Alona, gesturing with my hands, and I'm like, 'Guys, I'm so sorry.' They're jumping all over the place and I'm like, 'What, what?' They're dodging, they're diving to the ground, and I think there's something coming to hit us all, so I turn around, saying,

Above

Dean tries to pretend that Meg's hellhounds don't scare him.

'What? Is it a camera?' They're like, 'No, Ferris. Put the gun down!' Somebody ran up and grabbed it out of my hand and said, 'Do not point this at people!' I was like, '*Oh…*' It was embarrassing, but it was pretty funny."

More dangerous than a waving gun was blowing up the hardware store on the back lot. "Originally the story had some cans with rock salt and nails, and I said, 'Let's make this bigger. Let's put some propane tanks in there, too,'" recalls director Phil Sgriccia. "Randy Shymkiw, the head of the special effects department, and his crew did a really cool job with it. It took a long time to set up because of safety. We had to be four hundred yards away and around a corner in case pieces of nails and wood came flying."

Jo and Ellen could not have survived that blast, but it remains to be seen whether or not Meg survived her dip in Holy Fire. "I loved doing that scene in the fire," says Rachel Miner. "There's a fun moment where it looks like maybe Cass and I could kiss. What I loved about it, too, was the demon-angel dichotomy. It made it more fun to toy with that flirtation, because of course the demon would want the angel to give in to his lesser instincts." ⚜

DEAN: Uh, excuse me for asking, but aren't you kind of signing your own death warrant? I mean, what happens to you if we go up against the Devil and lose?
CROWLEY: Number one, he's going to wipe us all out anyway. Two, after you leave here, I go on an extended vacation to all points nowhere. And three, how about you don't miss, okay? Morons!

MUSIC
'Everybody Plays the Fool' by The Main Ingredient
'Oye Como Va' by Santana

SAM, INTERRUPTED

Written by:
Andrew Dabb &
Daniel Loflin

Directed by:
Jim Conway

Guest Cast: Lara Gilchrist (Nurse Forman), Malcolm Stewart (Dr. Aaron Fuller), Gwenda Lorenzetti (Susan Fletcher), Juan Riedinger (Ted), Holly Hougham (Wendy), Michelle Harrison (Dr. Erica Cartwright), Tanja Dixon-Warren (Night Nurse #1), Bronwen Smith (Night Nurse #2), Veronika Hadrava (Female Patient #1), Kevin O'Grady (Orderly), Claire Lindsay (Female Patient #2), Jon Gries (Martin Creaser)

After five patients are killed by an unknown monster, the Winchesters show up at Glenwood Springs Psychiatric Hospital in Ketchum, Oklahoma. The brothers tell Dr. Fuller the truth about the Apocalypse, which gets them immediately committed. Nurse Forman gives them thorough exams, then Sam and Dean locate Martin Creaser, a former hunter who called for the brothers because he's too much of a mental wreck to do it himself.

Dean has a therapy session with his psychiatrist, Dr. Erica Cartwright. Later, a sexy patient named Wendy kisses Dean aggressively. The brothers visit a patient who claimed to have seen the monster, but they find him dead with a hole in his head and his brain sucked dry. Martin figures out they're dealing with a wraith, which can be seen in a mirror and killed with silver. Wendy comes by and this time kisses Sam. Then Dean sees Dr. Fuller's monstrous reflection, and Sam violently attacks the man with a silver letter opener, but it doesn't affect the terrified physician.

Dean realizes that seeing Dr. Fuller as a monster was a hallucination and that Dr. Cartwright is also a hallucination. Sam is hallucinating too, and fights with imaginary foes, which results in him being restrained in a rubber room. Dean figures the wraith poisoned him and Sam with its saliva, so he and Martin go after Wendy, the obvious choice for the wraith — only to find Nurse Forman using a bone spur to suck the girl's brains out. The wraith escapes and goes after Sam, but just as she's about to pierce Sam's skull, Dean catches up to her and breaks off her spur, then jams the silver letter opener into her chest, killing her. As the brothers sneak away, Sam confesses he is angry all the time, but Dean tells him to bury his issues or he'll end up like Martin.

DID YOU KNOW?

Lara Gilchrist also played the character Holly in season one's 'Scarecrow'. It seems the pagan scarecrow didn't actually kill her — it turned her into a wraith!

DR. FULLER: To be frank, the relationship that you have with your brother seems dangerously co-dependent. I think a little time apart will do you both good.

"It was a nice surprise that you really couldn't tell who the culprit was in 'Sam, Interrupted'," says composer Jay Gruska. "The thing that stood out from my perspective was making the sound of craziness. I used off-notes, bold cymbals, bold guitar strings, and tried to make sounds that were not straight down the pipe. I also used some voices mixed in there, like when Dean is flipping out as he's walking down the hallway — it's like a cuckoo clock in his head."

Above

The stage is set for Dr. Fuller and Susan Fletcher.

DID YOU KNOW?

The title is a reference to the movie *Girl, Interrupted*, which explores life inside a psychiatric hospital. *Supernatural*'s Misha Collins appeared in that film as the character Tony.

"The fact that the doctor Dean is dealing with, Erica Cartwright, is in his imagination, I never saw that coming, so that was a great twist for me," says director Jim Conway. "Michelle Harrison is a wonderful actress, and when you realize she never existed it's a fantastic moment. I also love when Sam's fighting all those people and then suddenly they're all gone. Stuff like that is hard to do, but great fun. For budgetary reasons, I couldn't have those people speak — they were just extras — so it was very hard to sell the fact that Sam was being closed in on by everybody, but it all came together, and I thought it was very effective."

Before Sam lost his mind, he got his hands on someone else's, but the brain he pulled out didn't come from Schminken Studio as would be expected. "The show was over budget," explains Conway, "so Craig Matheson, the production manager, gave the brain to the prop department." So, as property master Chris Cooper reveals, they "spent thirty-five dollars on that one. It was basically a bargain basement brain that we manipulated to give it the desecrated look. We kind of pulled it all in from the cerebral cortex and stitched it and then took a torch to it and gave it that extra color."

However, the prosthetics shop did supply the skull cap for the scene where Sam cuts the top of the dead man's head off, "and then it was a visual effect split-screen as Sam reached in and took the brain out," adds Conway. "We just had to be careful that his fingers didn't go outside where the skull was when he reached in and pulled out the brain with all the gack dripping off of it," says visual effects supervisor Ivan Hayden. "We giggled a lot at that."

The big job for Toby Lindala, head of special makeup effects, was the wraith. "The monster that Toby did for 'Sam, Interrupted' was brilliant," Conway says. "In the original draft the wraith was there all the time when they were fighting it, and having done a lot of *Star Trek*s where you have characters in rubber heads, after a while it looks like someone in a rubber head, so I was really worried about long-term exposure to any kind of creature that's a makeup effect like that. We decided to go with only seeing it in mirrors, but Toby's makeup was good enough that you could've had that onscreen all the time. That was truly scary-looking makeup!"

"It's a shocking image," agrees Lindala. "The design of the creature, where her face was all mashed, the nose is rotted away, and the teeth are all set out with bare gums, was based on an extreme case of syphilis." What excited Lindala even more though was the bone spur. "That started out scripted as a long tongue, and people were humming and hawing over the practicality of shooting it and how it would come across visually. So Eric Kripke basically said, 'Toby and Ivan, I'm interested in seeing what you guys come up with.' We batted around some ideas and I was inspired by the movie *Rabid*, which had a great, crazy, sexual spike weapon, and that somewhere crossed with the *Terminator 2* spiked fingers concept."

Above
The eerily realistic set of Sam's confinement.

DEAN: You're my shrink? Lucky me.
DR. CARTWRIGHT: And you're my... paranoid schizophrenic with a narcissistic personality disorder and religious psychosis. Lucky me.

While the bone spur was disturbing on its own, it wouldn't have had nearly the same impact without Lara Gilchrist's wonderfully creepy portrayal of the wraith. Conway was impressed by her fighting skills, as well. "She happened to be very handy," he says. "She can throw a punch, and sometimes the hardest thing for actors to do is throw a conventional punch. She was wonderful!"

Conway also enjoyed Gwenda Lorenzetti's performance in the teaser. "That opening scene with the patient in her room and the screws coming out of the vent was just classic horror movie. The whole point there was to be as scary as possible." A great setting always helps with that, so it's not surprising when locations manager Russ Hamilton confirms that 'Sam Interrupted' was shot at "the shut-down mental hospital, Riverview Hospital, which we've used several times. We've played it as a prison, as a hospital, as an apartment, and, of course, as a mental hospital. It's fantastic. It's a very creepy place — it's not a place you want to be alone in at night..." ✑

SWAP MEAT

Teleplay by:
Julie Siege

Story by:
Julie Siege,
Rebecca
Dessertine &
Harvey Fedor

Directed by:
Robert Singer

Guest Cast: Debra Donohue (Crystal), James Clayton (Bartender), Patricia Harras (Donna), Lydia Doesburg (Katie), Ian Robison (Mike), Steve Adams (Officer Collins), Eileen Pedde (Mrs. Frankel), Greg Kean (Leonard Frankel), Daniela Bobadilla (Sydney Frankel), Alex Arsenault (Trevor), Jennifer Shirley (Ghost Maddie/Maggie Briggs), Colton James (Gary Frankel), Sarah Drew (Nora), Tanya Geisinger-McKie (Waitress)

Sam and Dean visit their old babysitter, Donna, who's having poltergeist problems. The brothers split up to investigate, and Sam is knocked out with a tranquilizer dart. When he comes to, he discovers he is in the body of a seventeen-year-old geek named Gary. Police escort him "home", where his parents think he's on drugs. Meanwhile Gary, who is now in Sam's body, trashes all of Dean's cell phones to prevent Sam from contacting his brother. Gary had intended to kill Dean, but instead helps him hunt and burn the poltergeist. Normally an underage loser who's allergic to wheat gluten, Gary takes advantage of Sam's body to eat hamburgers, drink alcohol, and have sex with a woman he meets in a bar.

Sam finds a book of dark magic in Gary's school locker, but is then ambushed by Gary's wannabe witch friends, Trevor and Nora, who tie him up. They reveal that they and Gary had planned to kill Dean because demons told them about the price on Dean's head — he's "Hell's Most Wanted." Trevor then summons a demon who possesses Nora, kills Trevor, then takes off to find Dean and Sam's meatsuit, now with a new, weak host who will easily be enticed into becoming Lucifer's vessel.

Dean confronts Gary, but the demon appears and knocks Dean out. Gary asks to be a real witch, but is told he must meet Lucifer first and say "yes" to his question. Afraid of the Devil and not wanting Dean dead anymore, Gary tries to exorcise the demon, who turns her wrath on him, but Dean finishes off the exorcism. Gary reverses the body-swap spell, and Dean warns him never to practice any black magic again or the Winchesters will kill him.

TREVOR: Everybody knows Dean. He's Hell's Most Wanted.
SAM: Oh, no. Have you idiots been talking to demons?

MUSIC

'I Got More Bills Than I Got Pay' by Black Toast Music
'Rock 'N' Roll Never Forgets' by Bob Seger
'Got My Wings' by Hazy Malaze

Rebecca Dessertine, assistant to creator Eric Kripke, contributed her ideas to the story for 'Swap Meat', and she explains how the episode originated in "a roundabout way. The idea of Dean and Sam switching bodies had been pitched to Eric at the very beginning, and fans have always wanted to see them switch bodies," she says. "But when it came down to it, the writers hadn't done that because that doesn't really work — Jensen acting like Jared and Jared acting like Jensen doesn't add a lot of

fun or excitement. So I pitched a certain way of doing the story. It was a little bit different than how it came out, but it was very much along the lines of waking up [in a different body] and you see yourself as the person that everyone else sees, but the camera sees you as your regular character."

The episode turned out great, but some people, such as executive producer Robert Singer, needed some convincing early on. "That was one where people were going, 'What? How does this work?' Myself included," Singer admits. "Eric kept assuring me that once you saw it on screen it would totally work. Then, when I got to Vancouver, everyone from wardrobe to hair and makeup people were like, 'What? How does this…?' You try to explain who's talking when, who's in the mirror, which voices you hear, and it really is a jigsaw puzzle. I was like, 'I trust Eric; he told me it would work and I believe him.' Then we all watched the episode and went, 'Eric was right. This works!'"

Right from the opening scene it was clear that Jared Padalecki playing the character Gary inside Sam's body was going to work. "He just killed that," says Singer. "It was great. He really got into that character. It was so funny, and I remember there was one take where he didn't say the line exactly right, but we kept it in because it was so funny. The line was, 'I would love to have sex with you, Crystal,' and for some reason Jared said, 'Crystal, I would love to have *the sex* with you.' I was like, 'Oh, let's print that.' I thought it was hilarious."

Above

Not the typical setting for a witch's lair.

That scene was filmed on location at The Buck & Ear Bar & Grill at the Steveston Hotel. "We shot that inside the bar and the fast food scene inside the diner [Steveston Café], which was next to it",says locations manager Russ Hamilton. "We turned this very generic-looking diner into Patriot Burger in about eight hours, and it looked great."

NORA: We were down here goofing around with that book—
TREVOR: Um, I wouldn't exactly call praying to our Dark Overlord goofing around.
NORA: Don't be a loser, Trev.

"We made the Patriot Burger uniform for Jared, and he was a great sport about wearing it," says costume designer Diane Widas. "The only thing that he wasn't down with was his little envelope hat." Maybe Gary lost it during the body swap.

The real mystery is which book the props department used for the spell book. "We buy a lot of old books, and sometimes we recover them, but often they're nondescript on the outside," says property master Chris Cooper. "For that one, I know we put all sorts of pages into an already existing book. We'll create pages for a book, insert our

pages where we want in the book, and then hand it over to our book-binding guy who will then give it a once-over and make it function better, being that it's an old book and we don't want it to fall apart."

Gary may have thought his life sucked, but it couldn't have been that bad if a girl liked him enough to see past his dorky envelope hat and dangerous dark magic hobby. "All the actors did a great job," remarks editor Nicole Baer, "but I was especially fond of Sarah Drew. Her turn from naïve schoolgirl to enticing demon was remarkable." ✐

BODY SNATCHERS

Imagine if you could swap bodies with anyone you wanted, who would it be? Composer Christopher Lennertz doesn't hesitate long before saying, "I'm gonna go with Clooney." Jim Beaver makes a similar Hollywood heartthrob pick with Brad Pitt, although he adds that he's actually quite happy with his own body.

Executive producer Sera Gamble bucks the trend by not choosing someone like Angelina Jolie or Jessica Alba. Instead, she jokes that she would choose *Supernatural* creator Eric Kripke, but then says, "That'd be perverse! It'd be weird for it not to be a female. Anyway, I don't really want to swap bodies with anyone else because then they'd have to live my life, and I'd pity them."

THE SONG REMAINS THE SAME

Written by:
Sera Gamble &
Nancy Weiner

Directed by:
Steve Boyum

Guest Cast: Matt Ward (Uriel), Allie Bertram (Girl), Luke Welland (Boy), Julie McNiven (Anna Milton), Matthew Cohen (Young John Winchester/Michael), Amy Gumenick (Young Mary Winchester), Juliana Semenova (Angel Girl), Daniela Dib (Devil Girl)

Anna appears to Dean in a dream and tells him she has escaped Heaven's prison and wants to see him and Sam. Castiel fears she is working for Heaven and meets her instead. It turns out she's still rogue, and she wants to stop the Apocalypse by killing Lucifer's vessel. She is going back in time to 1978 to kill Mary and John Winchester in order to prevent Sam from being born. Castiel wants to go after her alone, but Sam and Dean persuade him to take them. Castiel, weakened by the trip back in time, sits out the fight.

Before Sam and Dean can convince Mary that she's in danger, Anna lures John away. She tries to kill him, but his wife and future sons save him and send Anna away with an angel-banishing sigil. John can hardly believe that monsters exist, much less that his wife has been fighting them all her life. At an old Campbell family farmhouse, they set up their defences. Mary learns of the boys' true identity, but tells them she can't leave John and stop Sam from being born because she is already pregnant with Dean.

Anna and Uriel then arrive and attack. While Uriel beats Dean, Anna throws John out of a window, then shoves a pipe through Sam's chest, killing him. Dean watches Sam die and is helpless to stop Anna from killing his mother, but then Archangel Michael arrives in John's meatsuit. Michael smites Anna and sends Uriel back to Heaven. Michael tells Dean that his family's bloodline goes back to Cain and Abel, and claims free will is an illusion. Then Michael heals Sam, sends the brothers home, and erases John and Mary's memories, so that Sam and Dean's futures will go on as destined.

MARY: Devil's Trap. Pure iron fixtures, of course. There should be salt and holy water in the pantry. Knives, guns...
SAM: All that stuff will do is piss it off.
MARY: So what'll kill it? Or slow it down, at least?
SAM: Not much.

"I'm sure time travel is possible," states Nancy Weiner, the writers' assistant. "I don't think we have the technology for it yet, but I wouldn't be surprised if [someone] came

Above

Anna believes she can stop the Apocalypse if she kills Lucifer's chosen vessel, Sam.

up with the technology to do that." If time travel was possible, the choices of what time periods to visit would be endless. Looking back in time, Weiner doesn't know where she would go, but she says, "I'd definitely want to stay in an era where they have penicillin." Looking forward in time, Weiner has some clear ideas for how she would react if her children visited her from the future. "I'd probably react similarly to how Mary reacted. Sera Gamble and I both felt emotionally connected with that character when she finds out her children are hunters. I think my second question would be, 'What am I doing?' but my first question would be, 'What kind of life did I give my children?'"

Is it really that bad an idea to prepare your children for fighting monsters? If Mary's parents hadn't raised her as a hunter, the angel Anna would have killed her long before Mary rammed a crowbar into Anna's chest. "When they shot Amy Gumenick doing that, she was nowhere near hitting me with the crowbar," say Julie McNiven. "She was a foot away from me, but the way they edited it together, you don't really see it going in, you just see it as I'm pulling it out. They had this harness on me, with a screw that went from the harness through my outfit, and they literally screwed on the top eight inches of a crowbar so that it looked like it was going right through me. Then I took off the harness and put on my other clothes and when I pulled it out I was literally holding the entire crowbar. No CG, just camera tricks. I

Above

Mary tells John that she knows angels are watching over their unborn baby.

MUSIC

'Cherry Pie'
by Warrant
'The Creeper'
by Molly Hatchet

went home and told my fiancé, 'I had this line, It's not that easy to kill an angel.' and it's *so badass!*'" she says with a laugh. "I'm so not a badass in real life, so when I get to do that on TV, it's a lot of fun."

The tables were turned when McNiven got to jam a pipe into Jared Padalecki's chest, but unlike Gumenick having to stand clear of McNiven, McNiven actually had to hit Padalecki with the weapon. "He had a hard pad on his chest and stomach," she explains, "and I just hit it hard enough so it didn't hurt, obviously." Fortunately, there were no mishaps, but "There was something funny that happened," she confides. "They put the pipe that I stab him with inside a wall and created this little hole for me to reach in and grab it, and they set it up with this breakaway part of the wall so that it'd be easy for me to grab it and pull it out and stab him in one action. But when I went in and grabbed it, it wouldn't move! I was pulling as hard as I could but they kept having to break more of the wall so that it would be easier for me to grab it. I was like, 'I'm sorry! I'm weak!' It was really funny."

She might not be that strong in real life, but onscreen, "Julie kicks some serious ass," exclaims Misha Collins, "and I get two fainting spells," he adds wistfully. At least he didn't have to blow blood out of his nose, though. For the scene where she is suffering from the effects of time travel while fighting John, McNiven says, "They put this foam stuff up my nose on one side and on the other side they put a thinner

piece of foam that they'd squeezed blood into so that when I breathed out of my nose the blood would dribble out. They'd be like, 'Action!' and I'd be breathing hard out of my nose for several seconds and eventually it would trickle out. It was a very weird feeling. I swear you'll notice it too, because my nose has two bulges — I looked like a bull or something."

Above

Archangel Michael tries to sell Dean on becoming his vessel.

SAM: You're so beautiful.
DEAN: He means that in a non-weird, wholesome family kind of way.

Nonetheless, McNiven looked much better than the dead guy on the ground. "The first time I saw the dead garage owner it terrified me," says Amy Gumenick. "They burned his eyes out, and instead of doing it with special effects later, they actually built these eye contraptions that made him look like he had no eyes. They did a great job."

On the other hand, the dancers in the teaser were not at all hard on the eyes. But it's not the dancers that art director John Marcynuk hopes the viewer will never notice. "We actually used the Beautiful Room set from episode 422 in Dean's dream," he says. "Since it's Dean's subconscious, maybe he's dreaming about that place because he's really thinking about saying yes or no to Michael..." ✐

DID YOU KNOW?

If an angel wanted to possess you, would you say yes? "Definitely not," says Julie McNiven. "*Definitely* not!"

A Closer Look At:

WRAITHS

Wraith is a Scottish term for a ghost or specter, particularly one seen just after a person's death. Wraiths are often depicted as being shrouded in black cloaks, with their faces hidden and their sharp-nailed fingers protruding. Some witnesses claim that wraiths actually arrive *before* a person's death, as a portent of their demise, but perhaps what they're basing this belief on is Reaper sightings.

"Wraith is a name that has been used as a catchall for a lot of different creatures in various milieus," explains story editor Andrew Dabb. "We'd never had a wraith on the show, so we adapted that to what we wanted the creature to be.

"The traditional wraith is actually a spiritual creature rather than a corporeal one, but we wanted to do a monster investigation, not a ghost hunt," Dabb says. "We wanted the creature to drive people insane, and we wanted it to feed on brains, and there is lore about wraiths feeding on memories and emotions and things like that." What's more, legend has it that wraiths will die if they go too long without feeding on humans.

NURSE FORMAN WRAITH: I gotta say, you hunters don't exactly live up to your rep. I mean, Martin's a wreck, he's harmless. And you and your brother come in here talking tough about killing monsters? Kinda made you easy to spot. Then all it took was a touch, and you were mine.

"We needed an efficient way to get the wraith into people's brains," Dabb comments. "The initial idea was to do an *Alien*-type tongue, but the problem with that is that it sounds good in theory, but in reality it usually is more corny than it is cool. The only time it was cool was in *Alien*, and every time somebody else has tried it, it's looked bad. So then it became a spike. The nice thing about the spike was that she could use it more as a prop — she could lick it and all that kind of stuff. It became much more dramatic."

In its corporeal form, a wraith can give off the illusion of being human, but mirrors will reflect its true likeness. If you see one, it's best to kill it on the spot — silver does the trick — because if a wraith touches you, you will lose your mind. Don't go telling anyone you killed a monster, though, as that could land you in a psychiatric facility, and those places are wraith magnets — crazy brains taste better!

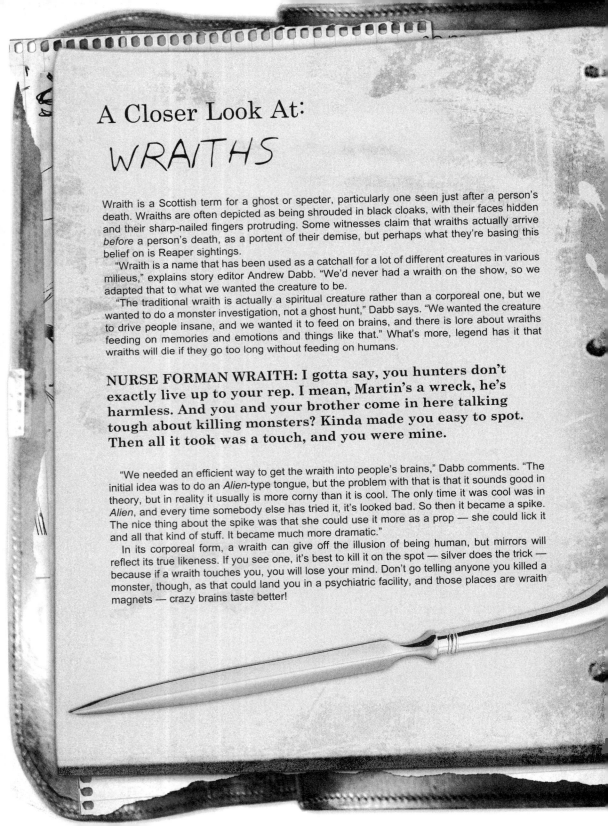

A Closer Look At:
ARCHANGELS

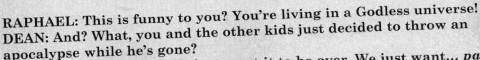

Angels are impressive. They can teleport, they have telekinetic abilities, can render humans unconscious with a touch of a finger, enter people's dreams, time-travel, even raise the dead — and if you piss them off, they can give you stomach cancer and remove your lungs! Yet, angels pale in comparison to archangels. Archangels are Heaven's most terrifying warriors. They can incinerate lesser angels with the touch of a hand or make them explode with the snap of a finger.

Lore across cultures and religions does not agree on the numbers and names of the archangels, but, really, there are only four: Michael, Gabriel, Raphael, and Lucifer.

Michael is the oldest and most powerful. He commands the Host of Heaven and is unwaveringly loyal to his father, God. When his younger brother, Lucifer, refused God's command to bow down before humanity, Michael did his duty and cast Lucifer into Hell.

RAPHAEL: This is funny to you? You're living in a Godless universe!
DEAN: And? What, you and the other kids just decided to throw an apocalypse while he's gone?
RAPHAEL: We're tired. We just want it to be over. We just want... *paradise*.
DEAN: So, what, God dies and makes you the boss, and you think you can do whatever you want?
RAPHAEL: Yes! And whatever we want, we get!

Despite being 'younger', Lucifer's powers rival Michael's. Among other things, he has found a way to control the Four Horsemen. He is known by many names, including Satan, the Devil, Iblis, and the Adversary. Lucifer believes humans are an inferior creation to angels, and is outraged that he was punished for refusing to love us. He created demons to spite God and would like nothing more than to remove us from existence.

Raphael is said to be responsible for signaling the coming of Judgment Day, which explains why he was guarding the Prophet Chuck, since the Winchester Gospels reveal the truth about the Apocalypse. He is no slouch in the power department, either.

Gabriel is the youngest brother. He was God's greatest messenger before he tired of his brothers' fighting, ran away from Heaven, and disguised himself as Loki, the Trickster. He can alter reality in any way he chooses, and as the Trickster, he had some very human appetites and a dangerous sense of humor.

The archangels are so powerful that not even the Colt can kill them. A ring of burning Holy Oil will trap them, and dousing them in Holy Fire will banish them temporarily. If you're really desperate to avoid them, you could always get an Enochian sigil carved into your ribs. It's likely only an archangel-killing blade — belonging to another archangel — can kill them, however. So if you've somehow angered an archangel, take heed.

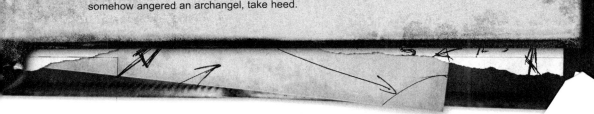

MY BLOODY VALENTINE

Written by:
Ben Edlund

Directed by:
Mike Rohl

Guest Cast: Jay Brazeau (Dr. Fred Corman), Colin Corrigan (Demon/Gaunt Man), Aili Storen (Alice), Andrew Halliwell (Russell), Michaela Mann (Jenna), Peter-John Prinsloo (Brad), Scott McAdam (Jim), Lucie Guest (Janice), Raahul Singh (Marty Khan), Michael Q. Adams (Cook), Cailin Stadnyk (Demon #2), James Otis (Famine), Lex Medlin (Cupid)

A couple on a first date literally eat each other up, and Sam and Dean arrive on Valentine's Day to investigate. Oddly, Dean's more interested in working the case than in celebrating "unattached drifter Christmas." Another double suicide quickly sends them back to the morgue, where they find Enochian sigils on the victims' hearts. Castiel explains that the sigils mean the people were marked by a cupid, so their target is a rogue cherub. The cupid is at a restaurant, where Castiel decides to eat Dean's unwanted burger. When accused of shooting poison arrows, the cupid cries, so Castiel reads his mind, confirming that the cherub only made the couples desire each other.

After looking into a death-by-Twinkies suicide, Sam attacks someone who appears to be a demon carrying a briefcase. The demon gets away, but the briefcase lets out a burst of white light when opened. Castiel tells them it was the dead man's soul and that the Horseman Famine is in town, making people hunger uncontrollably for love, sex, food, or whatever their particular unsated desire is. Unfortunately, Famine is making Sam hunger for demon blood.

Dean locks Sam up while he and Castiel go after Famine. Famine causes Castiel to gorge on raw beef, but claims that Dean hungers for nothing because he is dead inside. Meanwhile, Sam breaks out and overtakes two demons, then drinks their blood. Sam rushes into the restaurant, but it's a trap — Famine wants Sam to drain more demons. Sam exorcises them instead, then tries his powers on the Horseman. Famine laughs, but Sam pulls all the black souls that Famine had consumed out of the Horseman's body, weakening Famine so much that he is apparently destroyed, and leaving the brothers in possession of his ring. They go to Bobby's and Dean locks Sam up in the panic room for a demon blood detox. Outside, Dean screams to Heaven for help, but God doesn't answer, and Dean cries in despair.

SAM: So you were the one who found the bodies?
JENNA: There was blood everywhere, and... other stuff. I think Alice was already dead.
SAM: But Russell wasn't?
JENNA: I think he was, mostly. Except he was still, sort of, *chewing* a little.

The opening of 'My Bloody Valentine', with the couple eating each other, will likely go on record as one of the grossest moments ever on *Supernatural*. "It's the concept

of these two otherwise normal humans literally eating each other to death — along with the sound effects — that really struck a chord with people," observes creator Eric Kripke. "That was one that we always clapped our hands gleefully knowing that it was really going to be gross, but I'm not sure we knew that it was going to be as gross as it turned out. My wife got nauseous!"

Credit for making us believe the characters were perfectly normal people right down to the last bite also goes to the actors, Aili Storen and Andrew Halliwell, and director Mike Rohl. "That was really well shot, and the actors were astounding," says Toby Lindala, head of special makeup effects. "The intensity between the performers was neat to witness." Not that they were truly fooling Lindala, since he was the one who supplied them with the "flesh" they were eating. "At first we experimented with bread and raspberry jam," he reveals. "Bread's got that flop to it once it's wet; the texture is good. The bread soaks up blood like a sponge and releases the blood as it's chewed, giving us some nice dripping. Thankfully the actors weren't vegetarians, because we also ended up using turkey. It just had a little bit more of an organic flop to it. There were a lot of takes, and a lot of it was chew, chew, spit it into the cup, but some of it was fully devoured because the scene continued on. Still, it wasn't bad — they [ingested] maybe a sandwich and a half's worth each. A little bit of bread and turkey — Hey, we should've used cranberry sauce!"

Above
Castiel tethers a cherub that he and the Winchesters believe has gone rogue.

Above

The naked cherub (Lex Medlin) shows Dean his 'handshake'.

Lindala's sense of humor fits in nicely with the sensibilities of executive producer Ben Edlund. "The idea was, 'What would people do if they were *so* in love?'" says Kripke. "Ben said, 'Well, they would start eating each other,' which is how Ben's mind works; he just immediately went there. After a while, though, he was trying to talk me out of that as a teaser. He wanted to do the teaser of the people shooting each other because he wanted to start small and then build up to something bigger. I understand that impulse, but I was very adamant and I said, 'That is the coolest, weirdest, most messed-up part of this episode, so let's open with it and really make people nauseous. We'll *dare* people to keep watching.'"

DEAN: Is this a fight? Are we in a fight?
CASTIEL: This is... their handshake.
DEAN: I don't like it.
CASTIEL: No one likes it.

For those who weren't already nauseous enough, we next got to see a man ramming Twinkies down his throat with a toilet brush. "The distended belly was a fun piece," comments Lindala. "I got to sit in on the casting sessions to pick the person that was going to represent this guy. We chose this guy that had a good shape so we could build out on him, and he had a good level of hair and musculature on his body so it wouldn't look odd. There were a couple of other choices we couldn't make based on too much hair, too many muscles, but this guy had a great normalcy. We've done a whole bunch of versions of pregnancy bellies, but we wanted to make this distinctly different. It looked horribly uncomfortable."

Though probably not quite as uncomfortable as what Big Gerson's cook did to himself. "That was one of those things where everybody just gets giddy," says lead visual effects artist Mark Meloche, who was visual effects supervisor for this episode, as well as 515 and 516. "The cook dips his hands into a deep fryer in order to eat the fries. So when he pulls his hands out, Toby has this makeup job done on his hands which was absolutely disgusting. It was awesome! The hands were supposed to be steaming and smoking, and we were even talking about bringing blisters up on the hands, but Toby knocked it out of the park with those effects. We pulled way back on the steam to make sure we didn't obscure any of the makeup."

Of course, who's to say having your soul locked in a briefcase wouldn't be even more uncomfortable? "In the initial scripted versions, the briefcase bursts open and a glowing vapor comes out and travels right up through the ceiling," says Meloche. "Eric pared it back quite a bit, perhaps thinking less is more, so the light gag ended up being just a little bit of glow, the small semblance of an effect which is a fractal vapor thing across the top, to give it a sense that something is there causing the light."

"It takes some amazing imagination for what the writers come up with on this show, that's for sure," concludes associate producer Kristin Cronin. ✍

Below
Castiel tries to console the sobbing cherub when he realizes that the cherub didn't cause the deaths.

DEAD MEN DON'T WEAR PLAID

Written by: Jeremy Carver

Directed by: John Showalter

Guest Cast: Troy Ruptash (Clay Thompson), Scott McNeil (Benny Sutton), Ben Geldreich (Digger Wells), Aubrey Arnason (Hannah Thompson), Carrie Anne Fleming (Karen Singer), Chris Bradford (Owen Mills), Kai Kennedy (Sean Mills), Monica Davis (Old Mrs. Jones), Craig March (Blue Collar Man), Kim Rhodes (Sheriff Jody Mills)

When a witness claims a man was murdered by Clay Thompson, who has been dead for five years, Sam and Dean head to Sioux Falls, South Dakota, just five miles from Bobby's home. Bobby tries to get them to leave town, saying the witness is the town drunk, but the brothers find Clay at home with his family. He confesses to killing the man who had murdered him five years before, but the local sheriff refuses to arrest him and throws Sam and Dean in jail instead.

Bobby — who is friendly with the sheriff — bails them out and admits that the dead have been rising all over town for five days. The boys are confused and angry that Bobby lied to them, until he takes them home to meet his resurrected wife, Karen. The only explanation is that the Horseman Death brought the dead back to life.

Bobby gives Sam a list of all the people who have risen, and Sam goes to investigate while Dean stays behind to make sure Karen doesn't turn on Bobby. Sam is nearly eaten by an old lady zombie, then rescues the sheriff from her zombie son. Karen gives Bobby a message from Death and insists Bobby kill her — again — before she turns into a monster. Bobby does as Karen asks, before he, the Winchesters, and the sheriff fight an onslaught of zombies in town and in Bobby's junkyard. With the help of other townsfolk, the living triumph and all the dead are killed with headshots, then burned. Later, Bobby tells the boys that since he is one of the reasons Sam is saying no to Lucifer, Death targeted him to break his spirit or get him killed.

BOBBY: She was the love of my life. How many times do I gotta kill her?

"We got to do a zombie episode!" exclaims Jared Padalecki. "Everybody digs those." There have obviously been zombie episodes in the past — the monster in season two's 'Children Shouldn't Play with Dead Things' was a zombie, and 'Croatoan' had some zombie elements, and in 'The End' there's kind of a zombie apocalypse going on — but creator Kripke says, "We really wanted to do a straight zombie movie. We kept flirting with it, obviously, with those other episodes, but we figured we'd just go for it and finally do it. We don't have enough time on an eight-day schedule to make

DID YOU KNOW?

The title 'Dead Men Don't Wear Plaid' should not be taken literally. "We laughed about that," says costume designer Diane Widas. "As I recall, there was a fair amount of plaid, actually."

a pure action-packed zombie movie, though, so Jeremy Carver said, 'When these dead come up, they seem normal, and at first they return to their regular lives.' It's a really nice way to generate a bit of pathos and drama, especially when we started discussing Bobby's wife. We had discussions about a lot more dead people returning — we talked about bringing back Ellen and Jo [among others] — but we decided to focus on one thing to tell that story right."

One element of the story which may not have seemed quite right to long-time viewers in the episode was Karen Singer's looks, because Elizabeth Marleau, the actress who played Karen Singer in season three's 'Dream a Little Dream of Me'

Above

Dean and Sam meet Bobby's zombie wife.

"turned out to be very pregnant." Which raised the question, "'Can we get away with casting Bobby's *pregnant* zombie wife?' I think that would have been more than the episode could handle," says Jim Beaver. "I'm sorry Elizabeth lost out on the return job, but I'm so happy with Carrie Anne Fleming, who took over the role."

Beaver adds that 'Dead Men Don't Wear Plaid' was easily his favorite episode of season five. "That was the most emotionally difficult stuff I've ever had to film, and it was also among the most rewarding. It required the difficult task of staying in a dark and painful place for hours on end. It's just acting, but your body doesn't know it's fake, and by the end of the day, you're a physical wreck. But I loved it, loved the tender scenes with Carrie Anne Fleming, whom I adored. She gave me so much in those scenes, and it felt as if we'd been a couple the way Bobby and Karen Singer were. I only wish we'd had some make-out scenes!"

DEAN: Are you crazy? What the hell?
BOBBY: Dean, I can explain.
DEAN: Explain what? Lying to us, or the American Girl zombie making cupcakes in your kitchen?

At least we got to see Bobby fighting off zombies from his wheelchair. "It was fun to do action sequences in the chair," says Beaver, "particularly handing Dean the shotgun while he's pushing me, and having him shoot a zombie and hand me back the shotgun, all in one smooth move."

Another smooth move was giving Bobby's house some womanly touches. "We basically picked a lot of stuff off the floor, did the dishes, and gave it a fresh coat of

DID YOU KNOW?

On *Harper's Island*, Jim Beaver's character was named Sheriff Mills, and in this episode Bobby and the Winchesters team up with Sheriff Mills.

paint," says production designer Jerry Wanek. "There was already so much character in Bobby's place. When we built Bobby's we gave it some really detailed moldings and rich woodwork. There's custom-made wallpaper from New York, we have a wonderful fireplace, and we have great furniture in there, but you can't [usually] see it because it's all cluttered. So it was nice to see it in its glory, because after we built it we immediately had to take it to a place where we believed it was Bobby's. It was great to freshen it up." Then it got covered in zombie brains.

"We were told, 'Do whatever it takes to blow their heads off,'" states the episode's visual effects supervisor, Mark Meloche. "One of the parameters I gave for the stunt people was if they got hit to fall back away from camera because we didn't want to have to create CG insides of heads. Well, we had a stuntman that fell down the stairs, and there's a shot where Dean fires up and the zombie's head explodes and he falls right toward camera. So I sent an early stage of the shot to Eric, and he was taken aback by what was actually shown — the guy's leaning forward and there's nowhere to look except inside his head. Shaun Roth, our lead 3D artist, modelled the inside of a head with a jiggling brain and I was really happy with that shot. It went to Standards and Practices, and because it's not a human it went through. I highly suggest watching the still-frames as he's coming down; there's a lot to see in there. That was a blast.

"And that old lady grossed us all out on set because they had her mouth filled with pureed banana and she was drooling all over Jared and it was so over the top, and Toby's makeup was incredible. She looked *bad*," says Meloche. "I gotta say that was the best episode I've worked on because, let's face it, zombies are just cool." ✐

MUSIC

'You're One of a Kind'
by Fundamental
'Lovin' the Sin'
by Kid Gloves

DARK SIDE OF THE MOON

Written by:
Andrew Dabb &
Daniel Loflin

Directed by:
Jeff Woolnough

Guest Cast: Nels Lennarson (Walt), Kerry van der Griend (Roy), Lane Edwards (Mr. Baum), Jean Nicolai (Mrs. Baum), Laura Ward (Stephanie Baum), Roger Aaron Brown (Joshua), Chad Lindberg (Ash), Traci Dinwiddie (Pamela Barnes), Samantha Smith (Mary Winchester), Colin Ford (Young Sam Winchester)

Sam and Dean are awakened by two masked men with shotguns. Dean recognizes them as hunters Roy and Walt. Walt tells Sam he can't just flip the switch on the Apocalypse and walk away, then kills Sam. Roy doesn't want to kill Dean, but Walt doesn't want to spend eternity looking over his shoulder, so he kills Dean, too.

Dean awakes in the Impala, then lights fireworks with a thirteen-year-old Sam. Castiel tells him through the car radio that he's in Heaven, and to follow the road to find the real, adult Sam. Sam is eating Thanksgiving dinner with his eleven-year-old girlfriend Stephanie and her family. Castiel warns the brothers through the TV to stay away from the light, since Zachariah needs the vessels alive, then says he wants them to find Heaven's gardener, Joshua, who speaks to God. They relive other flashbacks and are nearly caught by Zachariah, but someone in a wrestling costume whisks them away.

The wrestler is Ash. His Heaven is Harvelle's Roadhouse, and he has become fluent in Enochian. After another reunion, with Pamela, they set off to find Joshua. They wind up with a demonic, yellow-eyed version of their mother instead. Zachariah arrives, planning to torture them, but Joshua saves them. Joshua tells them that God put them on the plane, resurrected Castiel, and even granted them salvation in Heaven, but He isn't going to intervene anymore, and the amulet won't locate Him. The Winchesters return to their intact bodies and brief Castiel, who returns the worthless amulet, swears at God, then leaves. Sam says they will find a way to stop the Apocalypse without God's help, but Dean doesn't look convinced. He drops the amulet in the garbage on his way out.

ZACHARIAH: Say yes, don't say yes, I'm still going to take it out on your asses. It's personal now, boys. And the last person in the history of creation you want as your enemy is me. And I'll tell you why. Lucifer may be strong, but I'm *petty*.

"Ash was a lot of fun to write," says story editor Daniel Loflin. "I'm glad he's in the episode. I really love his colloquialisms. I love when he shotguns that beer too — he does it like an old pro; it's so casual. I grew up in Alabama, so I understand that kind of character. I understand mullet people. It just felt very real to me."

"I thought it was a brilliant way of bringing me back," says Ash himself, Chad

Above
Zachariah shines a literal spotlight on the Winchesters.

Lindberg. "It was hysterical! I'm glad they kept Ash's quirkiness." Does it get any quirkier than declaring "Bud, blood, and beer nuts" to be the best smell in the world? "I think what Ash is relating to is the smell of home," says story editor Andrew Dabb. "To Ash, the Roadhouse is home. I grew up on a farm, so when I smell fresh air, tilled soil, and my grandmother's whole-wheat bread, those are the kinds of smells that mean home, safety, and security."

Traci Dinwiddie knew what she needed for her character, Pamela Barnes, to feel safe: her eyesight. "I said, 'I'm not coming back unless I get my eyeballs back!'" she jokes. She had been in the dark about her character's fate for long enough. "I went to a *Supernatural* convention shortly after I'd filmed 'Death Takes a Holiday', and the fans didn't know I was about to kick the bucket, and they were asking, 'Are they going to bring you on as a series regular?' It was hard to stay stoic during the barrage of questions. I tried my best to keep a poker face, but it was tough." At least she gets to smack Dean for putting her in the situation that got her killed. "That was great,"

Above

Sam wants Dean to still believe it's them against the world.

MUSIC

'Knockin' on Heaven's Door' by Bob Dylan
'What a Way to Go' by Black Toast

Dinwiddie says. "The *thunk* in that smack had me laughing like a hyena, it was so funny. Jensen Ackles said, 'Bring it on — hit me hard!' and I did — I really smacked him. After that take, I was so apologetic, but he was like, 'No, that was good,' as he rubs his head, wincing. He's such a good sport. He's like the brother I wish I'd always had. Oh, I shouldn't say that because I kiss him, but he is.

MARY: The worst was the smell. The pain, well, what can you say about your skin bubbling off? But the *smell* was so... You know, for a second I thought I left a pot roast burning in the oven. But it was *my* meat. And then, finally, I was dead.

"I don't think anybody was expecting Pamela to lay one on Dean," Dinwiddie adds, "but I think all the fans enjoyed it. The funny thing is, I know women who would probably pay their year's paycheck to have a go at Jensen's luscious lips, but during the kiss all I thought was, 'Wow, he tastes like Jolly Ranchers.' I don't eat sugar, so for me it was more about the sugary treat than it was about Jensen."

Whereas for Samantha Smith's first scene in 'Dark Side of the Moon', it was all about Jensen; she wasn't even supposed to acknowledge Jared Padalecki's presence. "There were a couple of takes where I did look right at Jared," she admits, "and it's like, 'Okay, I looked at him and he's not there.' Sometimes it

was hard to pretend he was invisible." Ironically, whereas on the show Mary Winchester couldn't see her son Sam, playing the character made Smith somewhat unrecognizable to her own baby boy. "He's a year-and-a-half," she explains. "I have short hair now, and when I wear my Mary wig he gets really freaked out. He doesn't quite get it — he doesn't know who that is."

Just think how you would feel in *Supernatural*'s version of Heaven — you would be pretty freaked out at first, no doubt. "Heaven was surreal," agrees visual effects supervisor Mark Meloche. "Whenever a demon gets sliced or an angel explodes or something like that, it's normally all grounded in physics. There's no such thing as fairy dust on our show at all. There's gravity, there's wind, all of that stuff. For 'Dark Side of the Moon' it was different because we were allowed to take things a little more over-the-top and a bit outside that reality-based environment that we were used to living in for the past five years. For example, the fireworks scene we pushed a little further — it's bigger and more glowy."

"We had to make that heaven suit an episode of *Supernatural*," says Loflin, "but I would love to think that a heaven exists. I definitely think more about faith and the afterlife, different religions, different gods, the evolution of religion, and things like that more now that I'm working on the show than I ever did before. My faith has definitely grown from working on *Supernatural*." ⚡

Above

Dean doesn't like Sammy's idea of Heaven.

DID YOU KNOW?

Chad Lindberg and director Jeff Woolnough previously worked together on the episode 'The Good Wound' of *Terminator: The Sarah Connor Chronicles*.

99 PROBLEMS

Written by: Julie Siege

Directed by: Charles Beeson

Guest Cast: Michael Shanks (Rob), Johannah Newmarch (Jane), Brett Dier (Dylan), Bruce Ramsay (Paul), Laura Wilson (Elise), Larry Poindexter (David Gideon), Kayla Mae Maloney (Leah Gideon/Whore of Babylon), Cindy Sampson (Lisa Braeden)

In Blue Earth, Minnesota, Sam and Dean are fleeing a mob of demons when the Impala is blocked by a burning truck. They are dragged out of the car but are saved by the Sacrament Lutheran Militia, who spray holy water before exorcising the demons with Enochian verse. The entire town has been overrun by demons, and the survivors have become devout followers of Pastor Gideon and his daughter, Leah, who appears to be a prophet.

Leah has a vision that sends Sam, Dean, Gideon, and others on a demon-killing spree. However, a demon hiding underneath the Impala kills a teenager named Dylan. His parents take it hard, but Leah promises them that Dylan will be resurrected on Judgment Day. She declares that the chosen ones will be given Paradise on Earth if everyone follows the angels' commandments (such as no drinking, no gambling, no premarital sex). The local bartender is not a true believer, so Dylan's mother kills him.

Sam calls Castiel, who arrives drunk because he's still despondent over God's refusal to help save the world. Cass informs them that Leah is not a prophet but rather the Whore of Babylon, whose goal is to condemn as many souls to Hell as possible. Only a true servant of Heaven can kill her, so they convince Gideon that she is not his daughter anymore, and he tries to kill her. He's easily thrown aside, but then Dean stabs her in the heart with a Babylonian Cypress stake and terminates her. Sam is worried that Dean is a true servant of Heaven now, and sure enough, Dean ditches him and drives off to say yes to Michael. But first he stops by Lisa Braeden's house to say goodbye.

SAM: Well, for starters, Leah's not a real prophet.
DEAN: Well, what is she exactly?
CASTIEL: The Whore.
DEAN: Wow, Cass, tell us what you really think.

Imagine you are trapped in a car, surrounded by a thick crowd of demons as they smash through the windows and haul you out. Even seasoned actors like Jensen Ackles and Jared Padalecki must have had moments filming that scene where they felt like they were caught in the middle of a riot. Stunt coordinator Lou Bollo had the stressful task of orchestrating that scene. "It had to be timed properly," he says. "There were stunt people shaking the vehicle and smashing the glass in from both sides with their fists. They had to grab the boys and pull them out, so we had to have that timing down pretty good." "There are just six or seven demons around the car,'

points out director Charles Beeson. The combination of the directing and editing make it appear like there were twice as many attackers.

As cool as the car scene was, editor Tom McQuade particularly liked working on the scene where Sam and Dean and several townsfolk were fighting in the house full of demons. "I love cutting action," McQuade says. "I take pride in cutting fights, because I think there's an art to staging fights and there's definitely a craft in cutting them well so that it shows the heroes in the best possible light and shows that they're strong."

Another great fight sequence was the climatic confrontation in the church. They were lucky to be able to do that, since film-friendly churches aren't always easy to come by. "Because of the obviously recurring theme on the show we end up filming quite a few churches," says location manager Janet McCairns. "We get some churches that are completely happy that we're there and they have parishioners who are fans of the show, right to the other extreme of churches that don't even want to return our calls because they'd be opening the door to Satan."

Satan wasn't in this episode, but his false prophet was, and that caused lead visual effects artist Mark Meloche to have to keep looking over his shoulder. "All our internet search engines have the safe search function turned off," explains Meloche, "so when you type in something like 'the Whore of Babylon,' you always have to be cognizant of who's actually in the trailer and making sure that no one's going to come in. We're all used to looking around at each other's screens and seeing all these atrocities because it's part of having to get reference for the beheadings and zombie faces and maggoty burgers that we work on. Well, you type in 'whore' and you get a lot of different images."

Even though Meloche has been aware of the Whore of Babylon for most of his life, a definitive description of her eluded him. "I did Catholic school," he says. "At some point

DID YOU KNOW?

When asked if he's ever done any découpage, Kurt Fuller replied, "No! And I never will."

I heard about the Whore of Babylon, but the only other times I heard reference to her was in off-colored jokes. We played with all kinds of ideas [for the episode]. We were taking it as literally as possible, like full-on blue eye shadow and big red lips and a big mole and making some kind of horrific caricature that looked like Carol Channing. Then we ended up paring it right back because our purpose in these shots is to be shocking, not to add a comedic beat, and just the name itself could take it in way too many comedic directions. So the shots in '99 Problems' where she shows her true form are brief and stylized; you only catch a very quick glimpse of what she looks like."

Maybe it was because of all the paring back of the shots of the Whore, but this episode was "a little short," recalls executive producer Phil Sgriccia. "We actually moved the Lisa scene from 'Point of No Return' into '99 Problems'. It was also the next scene, when Dean takes off from Sam after they killed the Whore of Babylon, so it seemed like a better fit to have that scene there."

JANE: I don't understand. How are we supposed to get to paradise now?
DEAN: I'm sorry. Pretty sure you're heading in a different direction.

MUSIC

'Too Hot To Stop'
by Marc Ferrari &
Steve Plunkett

It doesn't really matter to Cindy Sampson which episode her scene ended up in, she's just happy to be back on the show. "The coolest part about this whole thing," she says, "is that the first episode I did was in season three, so to get a call out of the blue over two years later saying they want me back on *Supernatural*, I was like, 'Awesome!' First I thought, 'Am I a demon?' Then I thought they were going to kill me!" Not even close (at least, not yet). Instead, "Dean showing up at her doorstop was a setup for what's coming at the end of the season," Sgriccia says. "Bringing back Cindy was great. She's always on her game, and the crew loves her."

A Closer Look At:

CUPIDS

In Roman mythology, Cupid is the god of love. Often he is more specifically linked with sexual love, and sometimes he is referred to as the god of beauty. Cupid is also known by his Latin name, Amor, and evidence points to the likelihood that Eros of Greek mythology is the same deity.

Cupid is usually depicted with wings, carrying a bow and a quiver of arrows. When Cupid shoots his arrows at pairs of people, those he strikes fall instantly in love. Not surprisingly, Cupid is strongly linked with Valentine's Day, the annual commemoration of romance, love, and affection.

Many people believe that Cupid's love couplings lead to fertile mating, which could explain why nude or diapered babies or young boys are often used to depict the god. Such artistic depictions were once commonly referred to as putti, but have now become interchangeable with cherubs.

While it is quite possible that there is a pagan god known as Cupid, it seems more likely that human sightings of and interactions with the angels known as cherubim have led to tales of a friendly, winged, chubby, naked guy with a baby-face flitting around bringing love to all he encounters.

DEAN: Cherub?
CASTIEL: Yeah. They're all over the world — dozens of them.
DEAN: You mean the little flying fat kid in diapers?
CASTIEL: They're not incontinent.

Cupids belong to the third class of cherubim. They can move around invisibly and mark their targets by touch — no arrows involved. Like all angels, they are winged in their true form. The first class of cherubim have been described as having the bodies of lions and the wings of eagles, and they are the guardians of places of import, such as the Garden of Eden, where they wield flaming swords. The second class of cherubim remains a mystery.

Dean Winchester feared he was dealing with a rogue cupid who was poking people with poisoned arrows. Fortunately, he was mistaken, but Roman mythology does warn that alongside the gold-headed arrows that Cupid uses to inspire love, he also keeps lead-headed arrows, which inspire hatred. In case there is some truth to that lore, it's probably best to avoid cupids altogether. Especially if they want to give you a hug.

Happy Valentines

A Closer Look At:
THE WHORE OF BABYLON

"The Whore of Babylon is mentioned a lot in apocalyptic lore and writings," states creator Eric Kripke. "Basically, she spreads false religion."

This creature can read minds and has the ability to take on human form. She tends to dress in purple and scarlet, and adorns herself with gold, precious stones, and pearls. The Whore poses as a prophet of the Lord, but she is a false prophet. Her full name, according to The Book of Revelation, is "Mystery, Babylon the Great, the Mother of Harlots and Abominations of the Earth."

She appears to be in league with Lucifer, since her primary purpose is to condemn souls to Hell as quickly as possible, thus adding to Satan's demonic army for the apocalyptic battles against the angels of Heaven. Indeed, she even works in collusion with demons. After making her targets aware of the existence of demons, she then pretends to speak to angels, who forewarn of the demons' movements. Then she sends out people to exorcise the demons. The so-called exorcisms are a hoax, however, wherein the whore has the hunters say some impressive-sounding words they don't understand — such as the Enochian version of "You breed with the mouth of a goat" — and the demons play along.

CASTIEL: The Whore can only be killed by a true servant of Heaven.
DEAN: Servant, like—?
CASTIEL: Not you. Or me. Sam, of course, is an abomination. We'll have to find someone else.

After the Whore seemingly saves the people from demons time and time again, they come to trust her "prophecies" as infallible. That's when she closes the trap. She says that the chosen will survive the Apocalypse and experience paradise on Earth, but only if they heed the angels' commandments, which usually involve things like no premarital sex, no drinking alcohol, and no staying out after curfew. The "good" people are then coerced into murdering any "sinner" who breaks the rules, condemning their own souls to Hell in the process. If further inducements are needed to get friends and family to kill each other, amazing promises are made, such as the resurrection of dead loved ones, untold riches — whatever it takes.

Lore has it that the false prophet is closely affiliated with the anti-Christ, so it's a good thing Dean Winchester ganked her before she could spin her web of lies around young Jesse Turner.

Keep an eye out in case the Whore isn't actually dead. Use a stake from a Babylonian Cypress to kill her, and tell her, "You die with the scream of a donkey." (It's funnier in Enochian.)

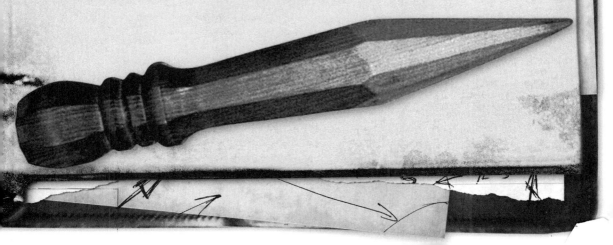

POINT OF NO RETURN

Written by:
Jeremy Carver

Directed by:
Phil Sgriccia

Guest Cast: Jake Abel (Adam Milligan), Michael Robinson (Stuart Holmes), Jason Wade Vaisvila (Street Preacher)

Opposite

Castiel holds everyone's attention, including a recently-resurrected Adam (Jake Abel).

Dean is in a motel packing his leather jacket, favorite pistol, and the Impala keys into a box addressed to Bobby when Sam walks in unexpectedly. Dean is still determined to be Michael's vessel, so Castiel appears and teleports them to Bobby's. Bobby reminds Dean that he hasn't put a bullet in his own head because he promised Dean he wouldn't, but Dean has lost hope and sees no other way to stop Lucifer.

Castiel overhears an angel communication, vanishes, then returns with Adam, Sam and Dean's half-brother. Adam has been resurrected to be Michael's vessel, but Dean doesn't want him to suffer in his place, and sneaks away. When Dean uses a street preacher to contact the angels, Castiel intercepts the message, then beats the crap out of Dean for betraying Castiel after he had rebelled for Dean. Castiel returns Dean to Bobby's, but in the meantime Adam has slipped away because Zachariah promised him a reunion with his mother after Michael has finished with him.

When Adam gets to the Beautiful Room — in Van Nuys, California — Zachariah reveals that he is just bait to lure Dean there. It works when Sam trustingly brings Dean along on the rescue, which Castiel facilitates by carving the Enochian banishing sigil into his own chest and clearing away the angel guarding the room. Zachariah stops the brothers from escaping and causes Adam and Sam to cough up blood. Defeated, Dean says to call Michael down, but then looks at Sam and changes his mind. Dean kills Zachariah with an angel-killing blade, then escapes with Sam, but Michael disappears with Adam. Dean has decided he doesn't want to let Sam down, so screw destiny.

DEAN: Word to the wise: don't piss off the nerd angels.

"The big fight where Jensen Ackles was squaring off with Misha Collins stands out for me in season five," says stunt coordinator Lou Bollo. "It was a really brutal fight where Jensen doesn't even get a punch in." This fight also stands out for Ackles, who says, "Misha takes me and throws me up against a wall, throws me up against another wall, another wall, and another wall, then hits me, and then kicks me into

a giant fence. I really go flying into that fence. They had my stunt double there, but I was like, 'I'll do it. Just lay a pad down on the ground.' I ran as fast as I could, jumped, and went *boom* off the fence and landed on the ground. I got up and was like, 'Please tell me we got that, because I don't know if I've got any more in me.'"

"Even with that one-inch foam pad there, he still got a blue spot on his hip," notes Bollo, "but he took all the hits. He didn't want to put a double in there because a lot of the shots were really tight. He literally took a run at that mesh fence, ran straight at it from about fifteen feet away, and if he hadn't controlled himself when he hit it he would've bounced another ten feet out from it and missed the pad. That was a fun fight. Then we had Castiel fight a couple of angel punks who were trying to get him as he was pulling Adam out of the ground. Misha did a rather complicated knife fight there with those guys. Normally when our guys fight they have a specific style, which is down-and-dirty — 'I'm gonna punch your teeth out and stick a knife in ya and I'm gonna do whatever I can to win' type thing. Whereas these angels all have those really long, shiny chrome knives, so there are blades going over people's heads, there's a blade coming through a coat, and all that. A lot of rehearsal time went into it, and it turned out really well. I think Phil Sgriccia was awfully happy with that, as was Misha."

Ackles liked how they brought back Dean's half-brother Adam. "Jake Abel is a

Above

Dean decides to kill Zachariah with an angel-killing blade.

good guy," says Ackles. "His character was a unique idea." In fact, Abel didn't truly get to play his character until this episode. "With 'Jump the Shark' he wasn't really Adam, he was a ghoul playing Adam," agrees executive producer Phil Sgriccia, "so we had to reboot that character. The scene where they're all in Bobby's house listening to his story was fun to shoot because we don't usually get five people just talking. A lot of times in the middle of those scenes somebody's eyes turn black and all hell breaks loose, so it was nice to just have a sit-down-and-talk scene for a change."

ZACHARIAH: Hey, don't get me wrong, you've been a hell of a sport, really. Good stuff. But the thing is, you're not so much the "Chosen One" as you are a clammy scrap of bait.
ADAM: Yeah, but what about the stuff that you said? I'm supposed to fight the *Devil*.
ZACHARIAH: Mmm, not so much. Hey, if it's any consolation, you happen to be the illegitimate half-brother of the guy we *do* care about. That's not bad, is it?

Much better than the Adam and Sam choking on blood scene. "That blood was awful," says Abel. "It's supposed to be chocolate, but it's not chocolate — it's *nasty*. I had it gushing out of my mouth. They put loads of it in my mouth, and even when you spit it out it just stays on your tongue. It's brutal. I'm sure there's somebody who enjoys it, but it's certainly not me."

Certainly no one would enjoy having an Enochian sigil carved into their torso either. Fortunately for Misha Collins, there are pain-free prosthetics for that. "That was fun," says Toby Lindala, head of special makeup effects. "There's this great technology using transfer appliances that are made out of adhesive, so they hold up so much better than foam, gelatine, or silicone, and they go on reasonably quickly. Misha's appliance ended up being six pieces, because we didn't have a cast of him to work from — we had photos and color references and some general sizing, but we sculpted it on a stock cast and had to adjust our placement and configuration a bit to make it suit him better."

The question on fans' minds is: Where do angels go when they're banished? "I think I go to a cubicle in Heaven where I have to just sit," says Kurt Fuller in the voice of Zachariah. "I'm a middle management kind of guy, so I have a cubicle. In it I have a calendar with an infinite amount of pages, and I have to sit there until I understand what I did wrong or until someone figures out they need me again."

A more complicated question is: Where do angels go when they die? Fuller doesn't know the answer to that one, but he feels, "The tragedy of Zachariah is that he had so many tools at his disposal, so many things he could do, and he just couldn't pull it off. [His death] is sort of satisfying though, because he's really gone to the dark side and the dark side cannot win, no matter how powerful it is."

MUSIC

'The Man Upstairs' by Kay Starr

MIKE'S TRAVEL INN
COMFORT & CONVENIENCE AT GREAT RATES!

SAM AND BOBBY —

GIVEN WHAT'S ABOUT TO HAPPEN, I'LL BE SURPRISED IF THIS PACKAGE EVER FINDS YOU. BUT IF IT DOES, I WANT YOU BOTH TO KNOW THAT WHAT I'M DOING ISN'T ABOUT GIVING UP. JOHN TAUGHT US BETTER THAN THAT. THIS IS ABOUT TIME. WE'VE RUN OUT OF IT.

LEFT THE IMPALA IN CICERO. WHERE I'M GOING, WE DON'T NEED ROADS. I KNOW YOU'LL LOOK AFTER HER FOR ME. BOBBY — YOU'VE TAKEN MORE FOR THE TEAM THAN ANYONE COULD EVER ASK. THAT MAKES YOU AN HONORARY WINCHESTER IN MY BOOK.

SAM. YOU TOLD ME ONCE THAT YOU PRAY EVERY DAY. NOT SURE IF THAT'S STILL TRUE. PROBABLY ISN'T. BUT IF IT IS, GIVE IT ONE LAST TRY FOR ME. AND SAMMY — ONE WINCHESTER LOST TO THIS FIGHT IS ENOUGH.

HAMMER OF THE GODS

Teleplay by:
Andrew Dabb
& Daniel Loflin

Story by:
David Reed

Directed by:
Rick Bota

Guest Cast: Richard Speight Jr. (Gabriel), Rekha Sharma (Kali), John Emmet Tracy (Mercury), Keith Blackman Dallas (Ganesh), Duncan Fraser (Odin), King Lau (Zao Shen), Brian Calvert (Security Guard), Patrick Bahrich (Salesman), Sarah Porchetta (Vixen), Adam Croasdell (Baldur), Matt Frewer (Pestilence), William Phillips (Milt)

While passing through Muncie, Indiana, a storm of biblical intensity forces the Winchesters into The Elysian Fields Hotel. Nicer than their usual digs, its buffet boasts the best pie in the area. When honeymooners in the adjacent room bang the wall hard enough to dislodge some bricks, the brothers rush over, but the room is empty, and the front desk clerk claims the honeymooners just checked out. Sam tails the creepy clerk but loses him. Dean passes a room with an elephant in it, but upon second glance, sees a naked man in a towel. The brothers then notice the other guests are missing.

They eventually find them, terrified and locked in the kitchen's walk-in cooler, but fail to free them before getting captured and brought to a conference room adorned with a platter featuring a man's head and internal organs. Their captors are gods, including Baldur, Baron Samedi, Ganesh, Kali, Mercury, Odin, and Zao Shen, who have united to stop the Judeo-Christian Apocalypse by using the archangels' vessels as bargaining chips. Then Gabriel — whom the gods know as Loki — arrives to save the Winchesters and protect his adopted pagan family, including his ex-girlfriend, Kali. Unfortunately, Kali knows he is an archangel and uses his own blade to kill him.

Figuring Kali can use the weapon on Lucifer, the boys agree to be bait, but discover too late that the blade is a fake. Lucifer slaughters the gods effortlessly. Only Kali puts up a real fight, and Gabriel returns in time to save her. The archangels face off, and Lucifer kills his little brother, but Gabriel left a video for the Winchesters explaining that the Four Horsemen's rings are literally the key to locking Lucifer back up in his cage.

LUCIFER: You know, I never understood you pagans. You're such... petty little *things*. Always fighting, always happy to sell out your own kind. No wonder you forfeited this planet to us. *You* are worse than humans. You're worse than *demons*. And yet you claim to be gods. And they call *me* prideful.

Initially, there had been discussions about whether or not to have the gods look like their classical depictions, but, "In the end, they weren't walking around in togas and stuff like that," says costume designer Diane Widas. "It was like a business conference, but some of their mythology was brought into their costumes. Baron Samedi had skull rings and a skull tie-pin, the elephant Ganesh had a gray suit, and the Norse god Odin had a jacket with wool. For each one of them I tried

Above

A place to relax inside
the Elysian Fields
hotel.

to bring in little pieces of their history so that if an audience knew it they'd see it."

"I was pleasantly surprised that there were all these pagan gods in there," says Mark Pellegrino. "I thought there was just going to be a Western theological apocalypse. I had no idea that Mercury and all these other gods were going to be in there. It was pretty fun to deal some blows to them!" The most graphic of which was Lucifer ripping into Baldur. "They just set up a stand with a mannequin in Baldur's clothes, and they had me plunge my fist through it," Pellegrino explains. "It looked great." Pellegrino's only regret was that he didn't get to go up against Zeus. "I would've killed all of Olympus!"

Despite taking on the pagans and his archangel brother with seeming ease, Lucifer's meatsuit was looking somewhat the worse for wear, as reflected in the prosthetics Pellegrino had to wear on his face. "They put patches of latex on my face, and then they'd tear the latex open — which is kinda like tearing your skin open — to make these blisters, and then they'd paint inside those and paint my entire face and arms white, with red and blue veins," Pellegrino relates. "I would forget sometimes that I had it on and rub my face or scratch something and then it'd really start peeling off!"

Toby Lindala, head of special makeup effects, enjoyed working with Pellegrino, but the gag that stands out from this episode for him is the security guard's severed

head. "We just did an appliance on his neck where he came up through the platter," says Lindala. "We covered him in latex and used different types of adhesives and paints. The one thing that I wish I had thought of earlier was, while we were there I said, 'I wish I had a turkey baster' to apply the final sheen on set. That would've been awesome! Poor guy, though. We had a food stylist that had this amazing array of meats and organs — kidneys, tripe, liver and all that. She chose everything for color and texture, and it really grabbed your eye, but the poor actor had to have his face on the table with all that.

GABRIEL: Lucifer, you're my brother and I love you. But you are a great big bag of dicks.
LUCIFER: What did you just say to me?
GABRIEL: Look at yourself... Boo hoo, Daddy was mean to me, so I'm gonna smash up all his toys.

MUSIC

'Women's Wear' by Daniel May
'My Fantasy'
'After' by The Bachelors

"We did a similar gag with the severed arm on the cutting board," adds Lindala. "We had a hand model with his hand up through a hole in the board. Fortunately, it looked really appropriate to have the sleeve still on the arm, because the sleeve made it easy for us, which is nice because we didn't have to torture the actor. The sleeve just had a little Velcro strap underneath that concealed the blend. It worked great.

Above
The deserted lobby
of the Elysian Fields
hotel.

I've put people in tables and stuff before, and it's always a difficult conversation when you have to let an actor know, 'Well, here's your Depends [adult diaper], and hopefully you're comfortable and don't have to use it, but we can't get you out for at least six hours."

The severed head and arm were not the most disturbing body parts Sam and Dean encountered in this episode, but fortunately what they saw at the end of Gabriel's Casa Erotica video remained off-camera. "That was fantastic," enthuses Richard Speight Jr. "It was a clever way for Gabriel to sign off. Yes, he went out in a blaze of glory battling Lucifer, and that was cool because he did it the right way, and sad because he got killed in the process, but the porno at the end was just so Gabriel. He could've just left them a note or done it a million other ways, but the porno is so spot-on with his personality, his sense of humor, so I loved that he got to go out on his own terms. It shows that even when he's making decisions he wouldn't have made previously, the thing that made him Gabriel was still there."

The boys looked grossed-out by the end of Gabriel's video, but the episode got much grosser with the arrival of Pestilence. "That's one of the grossest things we've done," states creator Eric Kripke. "When it's blood or gore or people eating each other there's a part of your brain that knows that it's not real. But when people are sneezing snot everywhere, that's real and that's really gross." ✐

DID YOU KNOW?

Richard Speight Jr. sometimes refers to his character as "the Gabester," a combination of Gabriel and the Trickster.

A Closer Look At:
PAGAN GODS

What do gods from the Chinese, Greek, Haitian, Hindu, Norse, and Roman mythologies have in common? Archangel Gabriel. Sure, from a Judeo-Christian viewpoint, they can all be grouped together as 'pagan' gods, but it's not as if they all hang out in one pagan playground like the angels do in Heaven. No, as creator Eric Kripke points out, "They rarely gather like they do in 'Hammer of the Gods'. It's more like they're a family from Gabriel's point of view."

The archangel didn't approach them as Gabriel, though. He took on the Trickster persona and presented himself as one of them, the god Loki. "Gabriel ran away from his real family and joined the pagans, and he has great affection for all of them. So for him they're kind of his family, and it's another way to talk about family on our show," explains Kripke. "For some people, family isn't where you're born, it's who you choose."

Despite first appearances, there are many similarities between the pagan gods. Most of them eat humans, and even those who don't still tend to view us as nothing more than meat. Just because someone enjoys eating bacon, though, doesn't mean they don't love their pet pig... Many gods treat their followers well.

BALDUR: Now, before we get down to brass tacks, some ground rules: no slaughtering each other, curb your wrath, and keep your hands off the local virgins — we're trying to keep a low profile here.

Baldur (also known as Baldr, Balder), for instance, is the Norse god of love, innocence, beauty, and happiness. He champions reconciliation and is said to be friendly, wise, and eloquent. It is no secret that Loki is jealous of Baldur, but while Baldur's followers assume that is because they tout their god as the "best", in actuality it's because of Baldur's clandestine relationship with Loki's ex-girlfriend, Kali.

Kali (also known as Kalika) and Baldur make a good couple too, seeing as how Kali is similarly revered in Hinduism as the most loving goddess. Just don't make her angry, because Kali is also known as the goddess of change, especially the change from life to death, which makes her either a great protector or a terrifying monster, depending which side of her wrath you fall on. Kali can summon flames to torch her enemies, she can make people choke on their own blood, and she can bind people to herself by possessing some of their blood. In her true form she has dark blue skin, intoxicating red eyes, and (at least) four arms. In her dark goddess mode she is a vicious slayer of demons, which is, of course, a good thing.

The good thing about Kali's fellow Hindu god Ganesh (also known as Ganesha, Ganesa, Ganpati) is that he doesn't eat humans, possibly because he is part elephant, and elephants are herbivores. He can take the form of a human, elephant, or elephant-headed man. Elephants are known for their great memories and strength, so Ganesh is fittingly the god of education, wisdom, and success. He often carries a bowl of sweet

coconut dumplings (modaka), so it's not uncommon to find Loki popping in to feed his infamous sweet tooth.

Of course, no one can pop in and out as effortlessly as the Roman god Mercury (also known as the Greek god Hermes), who can move his body at incredible speeds. He is, naturally, the god of travel and commerce, and messenger for the gods. Attentive gods and angels can see a blur when he moves, but human eyes cannot perceive his passage.

Mercury often trades goods between gods, so he keeps in touch with Chinese kitchen god Zao Shen (also known as Zao Jun), who is always on the lookout for new ingredients for his culinary creations. Don't ask Zao to make turtle soup, though; he might take that as an affront to his belief in the World Turtle. Zao's domestic god proclivities extend to all corners of the home, since it's his duty to report annually to the Jade Emperor on the activities of every household in China, after which each family is rewarded or punished accordingly.

DEAN: Now, on any other given day, I'd be doing my damndest to kill you, you filthy, murdering chimps. But, hey, desperate times... So even though I'd love nothing better than to slit your throats — you *dicks* — I'm gonna help you. I'm gonna help you ice the Devil. And then we can all get back to ganking each other like normal.

Norse god Odin (also known as Othinn and Wodan) regularly inflicts psychological punishment on himself by predicting his own demise in the jaws of a supernaturally big wolf. (Perhaps that giant wolf is an allegory for the Beast, a.k.a. Satan.) Odin is the god of war and hunting, but also of wisdom and poetry, and is also the leader of the Norse gods.

So why wasn't the famous leader of the Greek gods, Zeus, invited to the shindig? "We stayed away from Zeus and Thor because we were trying to stay away from the gods with too much name recognition," Kripke explains. "Yes, Odin, Kali, and Ganesh are really well-known gods, but we were trying to stay away from gods that everyone in Western culture knows about because we wanted it to feel a little less obvious, more idiosyncratic."

If you do find yourself at a conference of the gods, with their personalities and the kinds of powers that they wield, there's not much to say, other than you're probably going to end up as the buffet, rather than eating it.

THE DEVIL YOU KNOW

Written by:
Ben Edlund

Directed by:
Robert Singer

Guest Cast: Eric Johnson (Tyson Brady), Matt Frewer (Pestilence), William Phillips (Milt), Carmen Moore (Doctor), Stephen Park (Mitchell), Mark Ghanime (Dr. Drake), Chris Shields (Dr. Keller), Rocky Anderson (Janitor)

On the trail of the Horseman Pestilence, Sam and Dean look into a swine flu outbreak in West Nevada, but they find no clues as to where Pestilence is heading next. Suddenly, Crowley appears. The brothers blame Crowley for getting the Harvelles killed, but he swears he believed the Colt would work on Lucifer. He has been spying on the boys and knows about the rings and wants to help them find Pestilence. He takes Dean to abduct the Horsemen's demonic stable boy, Tyson Brady, who is also the vice president of distribution at Niveus Pharmaceuticals, a company rushing out a vaccine for swine flu. Meanwhile, Sam tells Bobby that once they have the rings Sam has to become Lucifer's vessel, take control, and jump into the cage.

Sam nearly loses control of his temper when he discovers that Brady is a close friend of his from college. He is horrified to learn that the demon purposely set him up with Jessica, and that Brady, not Azazel, killed her. Brady refuses to cooperate, so Crowley gets word out to the other demons that he and Brady are "lovers in league against Satan," which means Brady will be tortured in Hell for all eternity if he's caught. In fact, a hellhound is already after him and Crowley.

Fortunately, the Crossroads Demon has a bigger pet hellhound, so Crowley, Brady, and the Winchesters slip away while the beasts tear each other apart. Brady tells them where to find Pestilence in exchange for a quick death, which Sam is happy to deliver (though maybe not quite as quick as Brady had hoped for). Later, Crowley visits Bobby and tells him he can get him the Horseman Death's location — in exchange for Bobby's soul.

BRADY: What is this?
DEAN: All those angels, all those demons, all those sons-of-bitches, they just don't get it, do they, Sammy?
SAM: No, they don't, Dean.
DEAN: You see, Brady, we're the ones you should be afraid of.

"Crowley is a really cool character," states executive producer Ben Edlund. "You could call him evil, but he really is just out for himself, which makes him among the more pure characters. He has almost no self-conflict; everyone else is just dripping with it, but he's clean as a knife in that regard. I think he's great." Fittingly, executive producer Robert Singer says, "Mark Sheppard is great. He's a bundle of energy. He's on the set all the time; you never have to wait for him. He's got a million

Above

Crowley (Mark
Sheppard)
convinces the boys
they're on the same
team... for now.

stories and is really charming."

There might, however, be a certain stuntman who wishes Sheppard wasn't quite so energetic. "When I'm hitting Brady with the crowbar, that's a stuntman in a wrestling helmet with gel pads stuck to his head," explains Sheppard. "The really light prop crowbar looks like garbage when you hit somebody in the head — it bounces around and looks like it's flexing — so I was hitting him with a weighted rubber crowbar. That's a hell of a thing to do. I remember Bob [Singer] was looking at me and went, 'Just take a big hit.' I asked, 'Can I try something?' He's like, 'What?' I'm like, 'Can I just beat the crap out of his head?' Bob said, 'What do you mean? Show us.' So I was *bang, bang, bang, bang, bang!* Bob said, 'Whoah, that's just really, really ugly.' I'm like, 'Yeah, it's nasty.' I was whaling on that guy's head for the better part of two-and-a-half minutes by the time we finished. I thought it was great."

Another painful-sounding stunt sequence was when the stunt people had to

Above

Sam and Dean are on the trail of Pestilence and Death.

pretend they were hellhounds. "It was a tough one," says stunt coordinator Lou Bollo, "especially for the stunt people, because they had to wear green outfits top to bottom, could hardly see out of them, and they had to dive through windows, land on tables, smash tables, dive through doors and walls and stuff, and do it without wrecking themselves." Interestingly, one of the stuntmen had previous experience romping around as a big supernatural canine. According to visual effects coordinator Ivan Hayden, "One of the stunt guys that were in there wearing a greenscreen suit was a werewolf in *The Wolfman*. We had [special effects coordinator] Randy Shymkiw with air cannons, rubber glass, and tables that broke and blew apart, and we did visual effects elements with blood to simulate dogs shaking and ripping and tearing and that sort of thing. The big invisible hellhounds were a stunts, special effects, and visual effects extravaganza!"

BOBBY: You're just gonna chat some demons up and hope they don't recognize you?
CROWLEY: God no, that could get me killed.

Another visual effect that Hayden was excited about was the CG flies that followed Pestilence around, including the ones that popped out of Brady's blood bowl. "That was pretty crazy; the guys all went nuts modelling them up," says Hayden. "We had to animate all the wings, fully realized fur, textures on their legs, the refractions and color hits on the wings, the retracing on the eyes and reflections off the eyes, and all

Above
Sam isn't happy
that Crowley doesn't
want him to go on
the demon hunt.

that sort of thing."

The introduction of the CG flies was actually bumped back from the teaser of 'The Devil You Know' to the end of 'Hammer of the Gods'. "519 was a bit short," executive producer Phil Sgriccia explains, "and we thought, 'Well, if we take the teaser of Pestilence from 520 and put it at the end, now we can tie in with Gabriel on the video telling the boys about finding the four rings. So we did those flashbacks to the War and Famine rings, and then as they drive away we introduce Matt Frewer as Pestilence with all the flies and the grossness in that sequence. That was helpful to finish that idea. Then we started 520 with the monkey lab scene that was from 521, and the ending on 520 where Bobby and Crowley have their discussion was also from 521. So instead of looking at each episode separately, we looked at it as a bigger arc of the Horsemen and the rings and Niveus and the Croatoan virus. I thought that it worked out really well."

Of course, Bobby didn't just talk to Crowley, he shot him. Twice. "Getting shot was really funny," says Sheppard. "I've always worn Ted Baker suits [on the show], so when I was coming back from killing demons and the pocket's ripped off I was genuinely upset. Then when we loaded four or five suits up with shotgun blasts, it was so sad to watch those suits get blown up."

Not that Bobby shed any tears. Jim Beaver says, "When I first read, 'Get the hell off my property before I blast you so full of rock salt you crap margaritas,' I thought, 'Well, there it is, the best line of the series!'" ✑

TWO MINUTES TO MIDNIGHT

Written by:
Sera Gamble

Directed by:
Phil Sgriccia

Guest Cast: Matt Frewer (Pestilence), Julian Richings (Death), Leah Gibson (Nurse), Christina Jastrzembska (Celeste), Paul Duchart (Doctor), Fiona Vroom (Nurse), Conan Graham (Businessman), James Tyce (Security Guard), Frank Ferrucci (Manager)

Dean is livid when he learns of Sam's plan for getting Lucifer back into his cage, but is distracted by a call from Castiel, who is finally back in touch after his suicidal heroics outside the Beautiful Room. Castiel has lost his angel powers — and needs bus fare. The brothers pursue Pestilence at a convalescent home, but the Horseman infects them with scarlet fever, meningitis, and syphilis. Castiel stumbles in, seemingly equally affected, but is able to muster up enough residual angel strength to cut off Pestilence's ring finger and get his ring. Ominously, Pestilence warns that "It's too late."

Back at Bobby's, Bobby "pawns" his soul to Crowley to learn that Death is in Chicago. Crowley then helps them again by pointing out that Niveus Pharmaceuticals is distributing a vaccine for swine flu that's laced with the Croatoan virus. Dean and Crowley head to Chicago while Sam, Bobby, and Castiel plan to stop the vaccine shipments. Before he leaves, Crowley gives Bobby his legs back as a sub-clause in the soul-pawning deal.

Sam, Bobby, and Castiel face some resistance at the Niveus warehouse, but they rescue some innocents, kill the demons and Crotes, and incinerate the vaccines. In Chicago, Crowley gives Dean Death's scythe to kill Death himself with, but the Horseman magically retrieves it from Dean's grasp. Then, over pizza, the ancient creature reveals he is bound to Lucifer because of a spell, then voluntarily gives Dean his ring, along with usage instructions, so that Sam can return Lucifer to his cage. Back at Bobby's, Dean is hesitant to tell Sam to jump into the cage, which makes Bobby wonder if Dean is more afraid of losing the fight with Lucifer or losing Sam.

BOBBY: World's gonna end. Seems stupid to get all precious over one little... soul.
DEAN: You *sold your soul?*
CROWLEY: Oh, more like *pawned* it. I fully intend to give it back.

DID YOU
KNOW?

For a while, the
working title on
episode 521 was
'Collect All Four'.

"'Two Minutes to Midnight' was a lot of fun to work on," says executive producer Sera Gamble. "It was like two episodes in one because we had to handle two Horsemen in the same episode. We had a lot of stuff to cover. When we realized that we were going to have Crowley make a deal with Bobby in that episode too, which I believe was a pitch that came from Ben Edlund, that became my favorite thing in the episode."

Of course, crossroads deals have to be sealed with a kiss. "Mark Sheppard was game for it," says executive producer Phil Sgriccia. "We had a good time with him. I

106   SUPERNATURAL: SEASON 5

shot it on an iPhone just off to the side, as if Crowley was holding his hand away from them when they kiss. I did multiple takes just to make sure that there was an ick factor for Jim and Mark while we were doing it! We had to put them through a little bit of hell. It was quite funny, and the crew was giggling the whole time."

Kissing Sheppard was "stubbly, and *he* was the one who used tongue," Jim Beaver deadpans. "No, seriously, it was a bit uncomfortable, mainly because we had to hold the pose for quite a while to get a good photo, and that kind of thing is awkward even if you're kissing a girl."

At one point during the shooting of this episode, Beaver probably wanted to slap two guys — specifically Jensen Ackles and Jared Padalecki. "If we get an opportunity to make things difficult for Jim, we definitely take advantage of that," says Ackles. "On his coverage, we totally changed all the dialogue, so he had to try to remember his lines without having any of the cue lines. When the cameras are off us, all bets are off, especially with guys that we know can take it. So a lot of times it's, 'Let's see how long they can last without laughing in a serious scene.' We'll change the words up or we'll start saying their next line before they say it, which really just throws people off. We like messing with people — we don't like them to

Above
Dean waits for
Crowley to find
Death.

Above

Dean and Sam are taken aback when Crowley heals Bobby's legs.

MUSIC

'Oh Death'
by Jen Titus

be too serious."

Even Death doesn't take things too seriously on the show, chatting about the Devil over pizza. "They were pretty good-tasting pizzas," Sgriccia says. "Jensen wanted to take one home with him at the end of the day." Sgriccia knows good Chicago-style pizza too, since he used to live in Chicago. "When I lived there, I had my favorites," he says. For the episode, "We found a place in Vancouver that called themselves Chicago's Deep Dish Pizza, and their pizza was as close as we could get, but we wanted them to make it an inch thicker than they normally made it, so they did it for us special."

DEATH: Lucifer has me *bound* to him — some unseemly little spell. He has me where he wants, when he wants. That's why I couldn't go to *you*. I had to *wait* for you to catch up. He made me his weapon. Hurricanes, floods, raising the dead. I'm more powerful than you can process, and I'm enslaved to a bratty child having a tantrum.

Another piece of Chicago that was created in Vancouver was the 'L' rapid transit

Above
Sam and Dean are
surprised at the deal
Bobby has made with
Crowley.

system. "We built the pillars that hold up the L track in Chicago in our back lot, because that's really hard to duplicate," says locations manager Janet McCairns. "We did a matte painting shot of the full CG train," explains visual effects supervisor Ivan Hayden. "One of the benefits of doing in-house visual effects is that our budget can be looked at across the whole season, as opposed to a specific cost for each thing. So where most shows would go buy a piece of stock footage for the establishing shot of Chicago, we get to do a CG train shot, which was pretty fun."

Property master Chris Cooper had a lot of fun producing the Four Horsemen's rings. "They're completely original designs created exclusively for the show and the characters," he says. "Everything for Pestilence is a pukey green, and we made the stone on his ring look almost like an infection, something you'd see in a microscope with the snotty green color, and the band is silver and diseased. Death's ring has a similar shape, and the stone is white as white. They're one-of-a-kind, but the design needed to be almost utilitarian, so that they're not something that really stands out; they're just guys' rings. They're not too big or too fancy, there's nothing about them that catches your eye, until you join them together."

A Closer Look At:

THE FOUR HORSEMEN OF THE APOCALYPSE

"The Four Horsemen are part of the Book of Revelation," executive producer Phil Sgriccia points out. "[It says] the Four Horsemen of the Apocalypse will ride the Earth on different-colored horses." Of course, as this is 2010, the Horsemen have upgraded their steeds.

"War rides a red horse, so we chose a red Mustang," says Sgriccia. Often War's horse is referred to as fiery red, but blood red would be an apt description as well. The Book of Revelation also informs us that War carries a great sword when he takes away the peace of the world and makes men slay each other.

Famine rides a black horse, which has become a black Cadillac Escalade. He has a pair of scales, and he tips the balance of man's hungers — for food, sex, alcohol, everything — to insatiable extremes. Famine's own hunger for souls is just as unquenchable.

Pestilence rides a pale green horse, which has become a sickly green station wagon. He carries a bow and arrow, used to spread diseases far and wide. Perhaps due to the high death counts brought on by Pestilence's plagues, he is sometimes mistaken for Death and is said to ride a white horse.

It is in fact Death who rides the white horse, or rather, a white Cadillac El Dorado. He is the oldest and most powerful Horseman. He can inflict death by any means — earthquakes, hurricanes, *zombies*, you name it. He carries a scythe, which can kill anything, possibly even Death himself.

SAM: So who are you?
WAR: Here's a hint: I was in Germany, then in Germany, then in the Middle East... I was in Darfur when my beeper went off. I'm waiting to hook up with my siblings, I've got three. We're gonna have so much fun together.

Aside from the scythe, the Horsemen's tools — sword, scales, and bow and arrows — are actually just symbols of their powers. Their powers, which seem to be part of their very beings, are channeled through mystical rings they wear. The rings also have an alternate purpose: when brought together, they form a key that opens a portal to the Devil's cage in Hell. Which is ironic, since Lucifer has risked antagonizing the Horsemen by binding them to him and forcing them to act upon his every whim.

"The Horsemen have varying degrees of loyalty to Lucifer," states executive producer Sera Gamble. "War and Famine seem to be very copasetic with Lucifer's plan. Pestilence is more interested in exacting personal revenge for what the Winchesters have done to his brothers. He'd turn over their corpses to Lucifer and be like, 'Patch them up.' As for Death, he has an antagonistic relationship with Lucifer. It's the ultimate version of the situation in season one's 'Faith', where the preacher's wife found a

supernatural spell by which she could bind a Reaper to her. Lucifer had a super-powerful version of that spell by which, millennia ago, he bound Death to him, and Death is really pissed off about that. Death is only doing things like tsunamis and massive forest fires because he's compelled to by the spell. Otherwise he probably wouldn't trouble himself with a planet of this size at all.

NURSE: Sir, the Winchesters are here. We should go.

PESTILENCE: Are you *kidding* me?

NURSE: They have a... track record with Horsemen.

PESTILENCE: You mean my brothers — what they did to my *brothers*. No, the only *reasonable* thing to do here is to take it out of their healthy young *asses*.

NURSE: We're under strict orders not to kill the vessels—

PESTILENCE: Well, if Satan wants 'em so bad, he can *glue 'em back together*!

"As for the rings," adds Gamble, "in theory, any one of the Horsemen could have handed theirs over to Sam and Dean. They just weren't inclined to help. Whereas Death would rather give up his power for a time than be manipulated against his will."

As for whether the Four Horsemen are super-powered demons, fallen angels, or something else entirely, "The things that the Horsemen represent in pestilence, famine, and war are like forces of nature and are states that humans experience all the time. So it isn't as though when Lucifer comes on the scene he brings these monsters with him that are unleashed that we haven't been experiencing the effects of all throughout history. It's more that he gathers them to him," explains Gamble. "We wanted to make sure that we touched on the idea that War had been around, that he'd been doing his thing in the Middle East lately. That seemed to fit the description of something more powerful than a demon and different from an angel. Death is different from his brothers again, because he's vastly more powerful."

If you find yourself in the path of one of the Horsemen, you're probably out of luck, but not completely. If you can manage to wrest their rings away, that will help, but there are other defenses you can utilize: War's hallucinations can be beaten if you're aware of them and keep telling yourself what is real; Famine's power will have no effect on you if all your hungers are well-fed; a hazmat suit will protect you from Pestilence; and you might be able to gain Death's favor with deep-dish pizza. Remember too that Death's scythe can kill *anything* — but even if you do manage to get hold of it, good luck hanging on to it!

SWAN SONG: IN DEPTH

Teleplay by: Eric Kripke

Story by: Eric "Giz" Gewirtz

Directed by: Steve Boyum

Guest Cast: Jake Abel (Adam Milligan/Michael), Cindy Sampson (Lisa Braeden), Anthony Harrison (Sal Moriarty), Nathan Smith (Young Sam Winchester), Nicolai Lawton-Guistra (Young Dean Winchester)

Chuck is writing the final book of the Winchester Gospel and describes the Impala as the most important object in the universe. The Impala's first owner drove around giving Bibles to the poor, getting people right for Judgment Day.

Leaning against the Impala, Dean tells his brother that he is onboard with the whole Sam-saying-yes-to-Satan thing. Dean acknowledges that Sam is not a kid anymore and says if anyone can beat Lucifer, it's Sam. But Dean wants to know if this is what Sam really wants to do. Sam feels that since he let Lucifer out of his cage, he has to shove him back in. According to Castiel, Sam needs to drink gallons of demon blood to keep his body from exploding when he takes Lucifer in, so they drain some demons into milk jugs. Omens — and Dean's gut — tell them the Devil is in Detroit, so they set off. As they drive, Sam tells Dean that if the plan works, he is not coming back from Hell. He makes Dean promise not to try to bring him back, because Lucifer could get free again. Sam also makes Dean promise to live a normal apple pie life with Lisa Braeden.

They arrive in Detroit and locate Lucifer in a sleazy hotel. Sam says goodbye to Bobby and Castiel, then chugs the demon blood. Sam charges over to the hotel with Dean at his heals. A couple of demon thugs bring them to see Lucifer, and Sam kills the demons with his mind to prove to Lucifer that he is ready to say yes. Sam pretends he will only say yes if Lucifer agrees to his terms, but Lucifer tells them he knows about the Horsemen's rings. Ultimately, this doesn't change anything, so Sam says yes and Lucifer transfers from Nick to him. Dean throws the rings against a wall and says an incantation to open Lucifer's cage. Sam steps up to the portal, but then he grins, revealing Lucifer is in control of Sam's meatsuit. Lucifer closes the cage, pockets the rings, and vanishes.

In an abandoned building somewhere, Lucifer lets Sam return to the surface of his mind so that the two can have a talk. Lucifer tries to convince Sam not to fight him anymore, to accept that they were made for each other. Lucifer claims he wants Sam to be happy and offers to bring Sam's parents back to life, but Sam says he doesn't want anything from him. However, Lucifer thinks Sam will want revenge on the demons who have manipulated Sam's life, such as a grade school teacher and his prom date, so Lucifer slaughters them anyway and asks Sam, "Are we having fun yet?"

Dean, Castiel, and Bobby watch the news, which shows earthquakes around the

DID YOU KNOW?

Creator Eric Kripke didn't want the portal to Lucifer's cage to be too flashy or over-the-top. Director Steve Boyum says, "People would bring up, 'Oh do you want lightning flashes out of it and sparking and all of that?' And Eric always said, 'No, just think a black hole.'"

Above
Dean opens a portal to Hell.

world — the Apocalypse is starting. Dean calls Chuck and learns that Lucifer and Michael will be facing off at Stull Cemetery, just outside Lawrence, Kansas. Castiel tells Dean that if he goes there all he will see is Michael killing Sam, but Dean has no intention of letting Sam die alone. Lucifer faces Michael — who is now wearing Adam — on the battlefield and implores his brother to walk away from the fight, blaming God for engineering it so he would rebel and bring evil into the world. But Michael is a good son and blames Lucifer, not God, for what has happened to their family. Michael thinks Lucifer is a monster and is about to attack him when Dean drives up to them in the Impala, classic rock music blaring. Dean gets out of the car and tries to talk to Sam. Angered by the interruption, Michael strides toward Dean, but Castiel arrives and throws a Holy Fire Molotov Cocktail at Michael, causing him to disappear. This upsets Lucifer. He snaps his fingers and Castiel explodes. Lucifer throws Dean onto the Impala's windshield, so Bobby shoots him, and then Lucifer snaps Bobby's neck.

Lucifer beats Dean to a pulp, but Dean doesn't fight back. He just keeps talking to Sammy, letting his brother know he is not going to leave him. When Lucifer raises his fist for the final death blow, he is distracted by sunlight in his eye, glinting off the Impala's chrome trim. He glances at the Impala and sees the green army man

DID YOU KNOW?

When Jared Padalecki, Jake Abel, and their stunt doubles fell into the black hole (which was actually a greenscreen hole), that was shot at about 120 frames per second, which is five times slower than real time.

Above

Dean holds the key to Lucifer's cage.

Opposite

Lucifer lets Dean think Sam's about to jump into Hell.

DID YOU KNOW?

Talking to Sam, Lucifer claims, "We're two halves made whole. M.F.E.O., literally." That's 'Made For Each Other'.

that Sam jammed in the ashtray when he was a kid. Then he gets a flood of Sam's memories, from Dean sticking Lego pieces in the vents to the young brothers carving their initials inside the car and them sitting on the hood watching the stars — a lifetime of happy memories, time spent with Dean, family moments. That gives Sam the strength he needs to regain control of his body from Lucifer. Sam tells Dean it's going to be okay, then tosses the Horsemen's rings on the ground and opens the portal to Lucifer's cage. The brothers nod goodbye. Just as Sam is about to jump into the hole, Michael returns. Sam lets himself fall backward into the hole and Michael lunges and grabs him, so Sam pulls Michael in after him.

Castiel, once again reincarnated by God, reappears. He heals Dean and brings Bobby back to life. Castiel plans to return to Heaven as the new sheriff to stave off total anarchy, but not before reminding Dean that he got what he wanted: no Paradise, no Hell, just more of the same.

Chuck writes that Dean won't see Bobby for a very long time. Bobby keeps hunting, but Dean goes to Lisa's, just as he promised Sam. Chuck writes, "This *was* a test for Sam and Dean, and I think they did alright. Up against Good, Evil, Angels, Devils, Destiny, and God Himself, they made their *own choice*. They chose family." Chuck types, "The End," then shimmers and vanishes into thin air.

Sometime later, Dean is having dinner with Lisa and Ben, and someone is watching him from the street — Sam.

SAM: You take care of these guys, okay?
CASTIEL: That's not possible.
SAM: Then humor me.
CASTIEL: Oh. I'm supposed to *lie*. Uh, sure... they'll be *fine*.

"The pressure's always on when you're doing a season finale," points out Jensen Ackles, "because they're always the big climactic ending to not only a storyline or

Above

Lucifer tells Dean he's been messing with him.

whatnot, but to the season itself. After shooting twenty-one episodes it's like running a marathon and then being asked to sprint the last mile. There's a lot of pressure, and I think that raises the level of creativity and raises the bar as far as what people are doing. Like, for the scene with Dean and Sam talking on the hood of the car, I did two takes and I was happy with what I'd done, but being the final episode, I thought, 'You know what? Let me do one more,' and that ended up being the better of the three. So I think that added effort and that added desire of making this a special episode is definitely something cool."

Something else that's cool is creator Eric Kripke's knack for predicting — or possibly controlling — the weather. "Eric wrote this big sequence with Michael and Lucifer at Stull Cemetery, and any way you scheduled that, it was at least three days' worth of work," says director Steve Boyum. "Plus, Eric wanted a specific consistent Sergio Leone look to this thing. So we searched and struggled to try and find a wide open enough space that we could actually shoot this in and have it be within our field of permitted work areas. Just on the weather forecasts alone, I thought, 'Am I going to get three days that match? In Vancouver, in March, what are the odds of that?' The odds are so weighted against you. In the week leading up to those three days — we had a Monday-Tuesday-Wednesday scheduled for the Stull Cemetery — the forecast varied where it was going to be rain one day, sunny two days, then sunny two days and rain one day, and it kept veering back and forth and back and forth. It all takes place in ten or fifteen minutes, so you can't have it raining in one minute and then not in the next. But it ended up being three consistently cloud-clear days,

MUSIC

'Carry On Wayward Son' by Kansas

'Rock of Ages' by Def Leppard

which was unthinkable. It's just the luck of Eric Kripke to pull this off."

As amazing as the Stull Cemetery scenes turned out, Boyum says, "The mirror scene with Sam and Lucifer is my favorite scene in 'Swan Song'. I cracked the mirror very specifically so that the vantage could move from one part of the mirror to another part to another part. That helped me tell the story, because the camera operator did a great job of putting Jared wherever we wanted his image to be in that mirror. I just thought that the whole scene was creepy and weird and unnerving."

The most unnerving part of the episode was probably when Castiel exploded, which was payback from Lucifer for Castiel throwing a Holy Fire Molotov Cocktail at Michael. "They were gonna have Misha Collins chuck it at me from really far away and try to hit me in the chest," Jake Abel recalls, "and I was like, 'Um, I don't feel comfortable with this.' So they moved him in closer, and thank God they did because the bottle *would not break*. It was sugar glass, but they have these double-paned ones so that you can throw them without them shattering in your hand, and it just wouldn't break on my chest. It's in the gag reel, so it was worth it."

"That scene has a certain kind of quirk to it, because I just didn't want everything to feel so heavy," says Kripke. "Michael and Lucifer were having conversations about fate and destiny, and I just had this instinct to puncture it, so Dean plays Def Leppard, and Castiel's dying words are calling somebody ass-butt. I just wanted to take the stink off the pretension as much as I could more than anything.

"Other than that, it was about giving it stakes. In the original outline, Cass did not actually die. I think Lucifer did that little hand wave and Cass goes flying into a tree

Above

Dean and Sam react to the news that Lucifer knows about their plan for the Horsemen's rings.

DID YOU KNOW?

Stull Cemetery is a real cemetery in Kansas, and there is a lot of lore surrounding it, including visitations by ghosts, witches, and the Devil himself. It's also said to be a gateway to Hell.

Above

Sam and Lucifer discuss terms for the Devil to use Sam as his vessel.

and he's knocked unconscious, but it was one of those things you discover as you're writing it. As I was writing it I said, 'He just burned Lucifer's brother and Lucifer would kill him! So it was very natural to me that Lucifer's going to snap his fingers and Castiel will explode. For Bobby, the same thing. You gotta make this feel like it's got weight. Sure, he does get an angelic get-out-of-jail-free card, but in the moment of the action, you can't pull your punches. You just have to go for it."

DEAN: Hey, we need to talk.
LUCIFER: Dean, even for *you*, this is a whole new mountain of stupid.
DEAN: I'm not talking to you, I'm talking to Sam.

Executive producer Phil Sgriccia agrees. "It was good to have that moment of, 'Whoa, we're clearing house,'" he says. Jim Beaver certainly "wasn't shocked" that they finally killed Bobby. "I think I secretly thought maybe I'd be the one character who never got killed off on the show," Beaver says. "But dramatically, it was a strong choice. I wasn't surprised or relieved to be brought back to life, because it's been clear to me for a long time that the producers have no intention of losing Bobby's character for long, unless they've got a really, really good reason. My job is to make sure they never have such a reason."

Almost as shocking as the deaths of Castiel and Bobby was the brutal beating that Dean suffered at the hands of his possessed brother. Ackles was glad that it was Padalecki and not some other actor opposite him in that scene. "It's always good to go up against him during fight scenes because we know each other so well," he says. "My left eye was closed, and I couldn't see his right hand punching me, but he helped me by saying that he was going to lead with his right shoulder to indicate that the punch was coming and that's why I reacted accordingly. If I was doing that [scene] with a guest star that would never have occurred to them."

"Jensen was such a trooper," says Boyum of the scenes where Dean's face was all bruised and puffy. "He was in that prosthetic makeup for probably six hours, and he had cotton in his mouth simulating the puffy cheeks, and he had blood in his mouth and everything else. He's so good at bringing tears when he needs to, so the hardest thing for him was the tears building up behind the prosthetic that was over the closed eye. They had to keep going in and opening it up and letting the tears drain out."

Above

Lucifer is waiting for the Winchesters.

CASTIEL: You got what you asked for, Dean. No Paradise. No Hell. Just more of the same. I mean it, Dean. What would you rather have? Peace or freedom?

Fortunately, Castiel fixed Dean up, having been resurrected new and improved by God. The big question though is: Is Chuck God? "We didn't want to give a hard and clear answer," says Kripke. "I think you can draw your own conclusion. We did try to raise that possibility. We tried to ask that question in a way that didn't get too pretentious. We wanted to raise the question and give a provocative possibility. We weren't interested in any character ever saying, 'Well, that's because I'm God.' We presented a little twist, and people will make of it what they want."

Above

Castiel Molotovs the archangel Michael.

"My character starts the season declaring, 'I'm going to find God,' notes Misha Collins. "I kind of rolled my eyes at that, thinking, 'How are they going to do that?' Like, *Really*? God?' Then they kind of resolve that in the last episode. I'm pretty impressed, actually. The episode delivers. In the writers' room, they actually were like, 'You know what? We're going to do the Apocalypse!' I would have thought, 'You know, maybe we shouldn't do the Apocalypse. That's kind of daunting.' But they did it!"

Similarly, Beaver says, "When we got the scripts for the last episode, I confess I read it thinking, 'How are they going to do this?' I got through it and thought, 'This is an incredible wrap-up for this season.' It's a great plotline, and innovative in the extreme, which is what I expect out of Eric. It's audacious. The arc ends brilliantly, I think. I'm always shocked at how well they get themselves out of corners dramatically."

DEAN: So then what am I supposed to do?
SAM: You go find Lisa. You pray to God she's dumb enough to take you in. You have barbecues, and go to football games. You go live some normal apple pie life, Dean. *Promise me!*

Now that Sam and Dean have averted the Apocalypse, how does the show top that? "Who's to say the Apocalypse is over?" Beaver counters. "I mean, when there's a boom that big, there are echoes. One of the interesting things about any drama is it's presented to the audience as this discreet concrete thing that has no prior life and no afterlife. The fact is you don't have an adventure in your personal life where

you say, 'Okay, that section of my life is over and everything from here on is new.' It's just going to be more of the story."

Some of that story will definitely involve Lisa Braeden. "I don't know how long it's going to last," says Cindy Sampson. "Nothing seems to last very long in *Supernatural*, does it? I don't think Dean will stay with me long. Love is a great and solid thing, and if we love each other, that's one thing, but I don't think it'll change the course and path of who Dean Winchester is as a human being. I really don't think he's going to be able to change so much that his entire life alters into being a family man."

The only way to know for sure what's going to happen is to tune in to season six. "I want to thank the fans for sticking in there for five seasons," Ackles concludes. "It's because of you that we're still going. So stick around for the sixth season." ✐

CHUCKLING WITH CHUCK

Robert Benedict has heard that Jensen Ackles and Jared Padalecki are pranksters, but he says, "They never pulled any pranks on me other than I've had some awkward experiences with them. One time I was borrowing something from Jared and he was like, 'Just run into my trailer.' I don't know if he set me up, but I go to his trailer, and when I walk in these big dogs are barking like crazy and I literally thought they were going to rip my arm off! I'm a coward, so I was like, 'Oh no,' and jumped out of the trailer and everyone laughed. I don't think that was even planned, though — I think that was just me being awkward."

SAM WINCHESTER

There's something in me that scares the hell out of me...

"**I** love season five," Jared Padalecki declares. "Season five was a lot of fun to shoot. Every episode, even ones like 'The Real Ghostbusters' and 'Changing Channels', was intense."

It doesn't get any more intense than playing the Lord of Darkness. "I like that what started as a bunch of ghost stories and urban legends and myths has become something more with the whole Lucifer and Michael vessels storyline," states Padalecki. "It's like Emeril Lagasse says: 'Kick it up a notch!'"

"I was really excited when I found out I was going to be Lucifer's vessel," Padalecki says. "I thought, 'That's *really* cool.' Granted, if you told me from the Pilot and 'Wendigo', 'Oh, by the way, you're going to be Lucifer in four-and-a-half years,' I would have been like, '*What?*' but they always surprise us and keep us guessing. I think it's pretty rad. It's great because it's a big departure from playing Sam. I think if I'd started out as something like a Devil worshipper and then I played Satan, then it'd be like, 'Ah, well, who cares?' but Sam wanted no part of it. I started out as sort of the college boy who wanted to be a lawyer who wanted nothing to do with anything supernatural — I was like, 'Let me out, let me out, let me out.' Sam thought he was cursed enough by having to go kill [regular monsters like] a zombie, much less having to be the vessel for Lucifer. So I think it's a really huge arc that I'm certainly blessed to have been able to play with and portray. It's such an interesting role, so I was really excited."

In particular, Padalecki's excitement grew after he got to play Lucifer for the first time in 'The End', after which he says, "We we're being led to believe that Sam was going to say yes to Lucifer. So you wonder, 'How do you get there?'" Even before reading the script for the last few episodes, though, Padalecki recalls predicting, "Sam probably is going into this Lucifer thing thinking, 'You know what? Maybe I am the only one strong enough to let him become me and try to get rid of him somehow.'"

Padalecki also enjoyed "exploring what the Lucifer angle did to the brothers' relationship. Obviously Jim Beaver's character too — seeing how he changed and seemed so sour and so dire and so pissed off to be in the wheelchair, and we wondered if he could get out of it." Which he did, of course, but we will have to wait for season six to see if Bobby can get his soul back and keep his legs.

Maybe Bobby can pray to God for help — or talk to him directly if he uses the God-detecting amulet which, Padalecki hints, Sam could have in his possession, since Sam was still in the motel room after Dean dropped the amulet in the garbage. The amulet would then have come full-circle, as Sam received it from Bobby in the

first place. "Sam was going to give it to his dad, but he gave it to Dean. Sam didn't realize what kind of significance it had," notes Padalecki. "So when Castiel said it's to find God, that it burns hot around the presence of God, Sam was astonished, and surprised that Castiel was going to try to find God. Like, 'What do you mean?'"

Of course, if Sam did retrieve the amulet from the trash without telling Dean, that would be just another of the countless secrets between the brothers over the years, and possibly yet another reason for the brothers to argue and briefly split up at some point in the future. That's okay with Padalecki, who looks forward to those plot arcs. The two actors do rely on each other's companionship and good humor to get through the long hours they work, but Padalecki finds the times when they work alone or with other people equally enjoyable. "I loved episode three of season five ['Free to Be You and Me']," he says. "It was when Sam and Dean split up and they were trying to go their own ways and leave all this Michael-Lucifer stuff behind. It's fun because Jensen's such a great actor and I have such a great time with him, but I use him as a crutch, and I think vice versa. We'll just go off each other, so it's really challenging to do stuff without him. We're just so used to working with each other — I mean, over a hundred episodes, eight sixteen-hour days each of work. It's gratifying and satisfying when you can do something without somebody you can rely upon really easily and still make it good."

Episode 518, 'Point of No Return', was *Supernatural*'s one hundredth episode, and Padalecki is justifiably proud of his part in helping the show reach that impressive TV landmark. "One hundred shows isn't normal for any show," he points out. "Most do not get to one hundred, so it's been an enormous accomplishment and wonderful to be a part of. Especially with Jensen and myself. Even though we obviously had a lot of help from people like Jim Beaver, Misha Collins, and my wife in season four, it's been him and me

the whole time, so that's been really gratifying. It's been a nice ride."

However, the ride wouldn't be possible without gas for the car, and that's where the viewers come in. "Everybody says this, and it always sounds so cheesy and clichéd," Padalecki acknowledges, "but the fans really *are* the reason that we're here. If we didn't have the fans behind us we wouldn't be where we are now."

Literally speaking, where they are now is Vancouver, British Columbia, Canada, which has given Padalecki a bit of an identity crisis. "Vancouver feels like home of sorts," he says. "I know it really well. I know it better than any other city in the world, because when I was growing up for eighteen years in San Antonio, Texas, I didn't have a car for sixteen years, so I didn't know directions, I didn't need to know where to go, and then I moved out. In LA I didn't really go anywhere; I just stuck around my neighborhood. But here in Vancouver we're on location so much that I've seen so much of the city, and I've had a car here and gone out on the weekends and driven to Whistler and Kelowna and Seattle, so I know the city really well. It still doesn't exactly feel like home, but I don't know what feels like home anymore. San Antonio or LA or Vancouver? But it feels like a very warm friend."

It's good that Padalecki feels so comfortable in Vancouver, as he is going to be there for at least one more season, and quite possibly longer. Like the city, he is just as at home with the show's crew, who he refers to as a family. One of the great things about the crew, he says, is "You get a sense from everybody that it's a group effort, that everybody is looking out for everybody, and everybody is scratching each other's backs."

Most importantly, Padalecki is still enjoying playing Sam Winchester. "The show changes so much," he says. "It's been keeping so fresh. I think season six is going to be really exciting." ⌀

DEAN WINCHESTER

So, is this the part where you kill me?

"At the beginning of season five, when we realize that Dean is now heavily involved with the mythology of the show, that changed everything," states Jensen Ackles. "I'm like, 'So wait a minute... These two brothers are now the vessels for the entire Apocalypse?' I didn't see that coming!

"Before, Dean was the Han Solo to the chosen Luke Skywalker, whereas now he's actually a big part of the picture as well. He always has been, but it was never really revealed until recently, so I like that aspect of it. I like the fact that both brothers are kind of the chosen one, as opposed to one being the chosen one and the other one trying to keep him from going dark-side. Now Dean's dealing with two very difficult situations. Not only is he having to keep his brother from saying yes to Lucifer, he's gotta find a way to say no to Michael."

It wasn't easy for Dean to say no, especially considering all Zachariah's tricks and tortures, and Michael's promise to not leave him a drooling mess when the archangel was through with him. Ackles, however, is thrilled to have been Heaven's Hero, and ultimately humanity's hero. "I've always been attracted to those kinds of characters — the reluctant hero, the hero that isn't perfect," he says. "Not the Supermans and the Captain Americas, but more like the Indiana Jones and the Han Solos and the ones that have a little comedy and don't always save the day in the classiest way. Dean's not a James Bond guy; he's going to get nicked up and bruised and shot and cut, and he's going to have a hell of a time doing it. I think that allows for a comedic aspect of what is a more dramatic character, and for me as an actor, I like to balance those two things."

Another thing that needs balance is Dean's belief in his brother. "It's a constant approval and disapproval relationship on the trust aspect," Ackles explains. "They want to believe in each other, but something always happens to destroy that. When that happens, they doubt so intensely, but in the same way, something always comes up to show there's still hope. I like this dynamic, this constant battle to define their loyalty each season. The back and forth is appealing to the audience, because nobody knows where their lives are leading to. It's a constant doubt: 'Are they a team? Are they planning something behind each others backs? Who is going to be the first one to change his mind?'"

Fortunately, that doubt never took root off camera. "Oh, yeah," Ackles agrees, "five years working together is quite a long time — either you can't stand each other by the end of it, or you're good friends. Luckily ours went the latter way.

DID YOU KNOW?

When Jensen Ackles first moved to Hollywood, his agent wanted him to use his middle name instead of his last name for his stage name, so it would have been Jensen Ross. But Ackles said, "Listen, if I make it, I want the name to do me proud. And it has."

"But it's not just me and him," Ackles points out. "We've been working with this crew of 100-150 people, and it's kind of a family. We've built up quite a rapport with everybody. We've met new wives, we've held new babies, we've watched people lose thirty pounds. We have seen a lot of transformation. I think we've had nine people move into their thirties, me included. A very common phrase we use on set is, 'Wow, you were much better in your twenties.' There have been a lot of milestones within the group. So for this whole show to be a part of each other's lives for five years is very unique."

Another unique aspect of *Supernatural* is that it wrapped up a five-year arc where most other shows would have found a way to stretch out the storyline once the sixth season was ordered. "Eric Kripke wasn't going to tap the breaks when he found out we were going to go an extra year," recalls Ackles. "He said, 'I am going to do the five seasons, I am going to knock it out of the park, and then we will figure it out from there.' My anticipation of the first script of season six is high.

"With the series coming to somewhat of a conclusion, and then to get to keep going after that, I think it opens a lot of doors creatively for the writers, the actors, and directors. What I'm hoping to see next season is [us hitting] the reset button. Sera Gamble said something interesting to me," Ackles reveals. "She said, 'We've already got our formula laid out for us, and that was the formula from season one and season two.' We're not gonna replay the greatest hits of *Supernatural* for the next two seasons; it's gonna be a totally different dynamic — there's gonna be new motivation, there's gonna be new storylines, there's gonna be new characters coming in...'

"I'll bet it's gonna be, 'Let's get back to what *Supernatural* was in the beginning.' But obviously there's a giant elephant in the room, and that's the fact that we know everything that's happened over the past five years, the fact that the

Sam's motel room in 'Free To Be You and Me'.

100% Scale

PURE
Rio Colorado
NATURAL SPRING WATER

Castiel's Sigil

ATTENTION: MAKE UP
HAND DRAWING SIGIL
PLEASE SIZE AS NECESSARY

Above: Design for the prosthetic sigil Misha Collins wore on his chest while filming 'Point of No Return'.

Clockwise From Top Left: Sign used in 'Swan Song'. Zao Shen tattoo from 'Hammer of the Gods'. Label for bottled water used in the convenience store scene in 'Good God, Y'all'. Label for the snack food advertised during the Japanese game show in 'Changing Channels'.

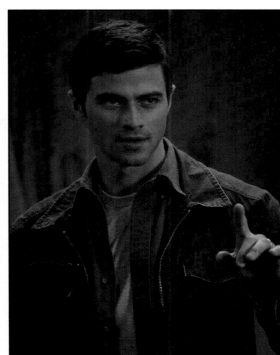

Diner set for 'Dead Men Don't Wear Plaid'.

The *Supernatural* backlot decorated in post-apocalyptic style for 'The End'.

A close-up look at Dean's amulet.

A priceless Castiel collectible toy.

Apocalypse happened. It's gonna be, 'How do you deal with that and still live a seemingly normal life in the *Supernatural* world?' I mean, we've known five years of these guys and what they've been through, and now they're back to almost where they were at the beginning of season one, which to me is exciting. It is like you don't have to reinvent yourself, but you get to take everything that the audience knows and everything that you know about these characters and now apply it to a completely different situation."

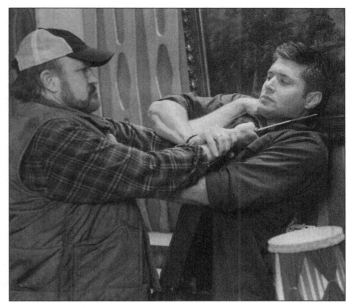

Regardless of where the season six storylines go, Ackles is just happy to still be playing Dean Winchester. "A lot of people say, 'You don't know what you have until it's gone.' Well, I know what I have," he says. "I know that this is a great show, a great crew, and the characters are well-written. I love my character. I love playing Dean."

There is one potential downfall to playing one character for so long — the lines between Jensen and Dean could begin to blur. "Jared and I do joke about the fact that we've been Sam and Dean Winchester over the past five years more than we have been ourselves," Ackles shares. "I don't know if that is a loss of identity or what, but it is a unique situation."

Nonetheless, Ackles adds, "I would venture to say that Dean and Jensen have become a little more separate, actually. Dean reacts to situations so different than me. In the beginning, we were very alike, because I didn't know who Dean really was, so he was me on screen. With time, the writers, Eric, and I were defining this guy and, believe me, now he speaks and thinks so differently from the first season and from me. He's tough and funny as well. He's the guy who almost every time gets the girl. My relationship with him has changed a lot and always surprises me; now everything seems new to me."

Everything about living an apple-pie life is new for Dean as well. "The way we ended, with that last shot of Dean, it makes you wonder, 'What the hell's gonna happen next?'" muses Ackles. "I like the fact that the episode wraps up the five year arc, but then it also starts us on a new journey. The fact that in two weeks Bobby is going to be off fighting a rougarou and Dean's not going to be there is almost like a massive control-alt-delete, and it's back to normal, it's back to the basics."

"I'm very happy that we got picked up for season six," Ackles concludes, "because I want to see where they go after this."

CASTIEL

The voice says I'm almost out of minutes.

"At the end of season four, Castiel broke with his superiors in Heaven and became a rogue angel [in season five]," notes Misha Collins. "Castiel has become more empathetic to humans, more personally connected to them. He has also become more human himself, and I'd say, by extension, less angelic. It's been a long, slow fall from grace for Castiel. The end result is that he's quite the husk of an angel by the end of season five.

"Over the course of the season he experiences, more and more, what it's like to be human," Collins elaborates. "It's an interesting question: 'What does it mean to be human?' Not many roles allow you to explore that in-depth." Of course, since this is *Supernatural*, that question wasn't explored in quite the way Collins expected.

"When the season started, I had this idea that they were going to do something along the lines of what Wim Wenders did in *Wings of Desire*, where Bruno Ganz is an angel who falls, and this angel, who'd never experienced the joys of what it is to be a human being, experiences the wind in his face, a hot cup of coffee, sexual desire, and things like that for the first time. So in the beginning of the season, I thought, 'Oh, this is going to be cool. Castiel is going to experience what Bruno Ganz experienced. He's going to feel the magic of being alive as a human being.' I thought we were going to have an opportunity to explore all that, but what the writers on *Supernatural* ended up doing was taking the opposite side of that coin and made it not the joys of being human that Castiel gets to experience, but all the suffering and misery and pain, like insatiable hunger, drunkenness, unsatisfied sexual desires, and the general feeling of being alone in the universe. It's all the crap of being alive. I was pleasantly surprised with that direction. Castiel got to explore the darker side of what it means to be a human, and I think that that was a very smart and interesting choice on the writers' part."

Another interesting choice was making Castiel a hippie in 'The End'. Short of turning evil like his brother Lucifer, Castiel was about as far from being a stereotypical angel as you could get in that hypothetical-future episode, where he buried himself in women and decadence. "That was fun!" Collins enthuses. "I got to play a different version of Castiel, and it's always fun to stretch out like that. I liked 'The End' a lot. It was simply epic, and I think the most apocalyptic of all the episodes of the season."

Of course, almost the whole season is apocalyptic in one way or another, and a lot of that comes from actual Bible lore, which piqued Collins' interest. "It's such a rich thing to draw on," he comments. "It seems like two years ago or so they really started to use the Bible a lot. Eric Kripke told me they have a rule that any mythology they

are bringing onto the show has to be 'Googleable,' which means it is not completely made up in their heads — any sort of mythological character or supernatural being has to be somewhere out in the lore already, and they are drawing on that. It suddenly dawned on Eric one day, 'Wait a minute, there is this other resource that we can be drawing on which is the Old and New Testaments. There is a lot of really fascinating stuff to draw on.' It is amazing how much of what's happening in the show's apocalypse this year comes from the Book of Revelation. I mean, [according to the Bible] it's some pretty out there stuff that is going to happen."

More "out there" than a rogue angel shouting out, "Hey, ass-butt," while throwing a holy Molotov cocktail at Archangel Michael? Regardless of what is prophesized to happen in the real world, Castiel has done his part in helping defeat Heaven's plans for humanity's destiny on the show. So now that Lucifer is back in his cage and Castiel has got his full angel mojo back, will Castiel's personality morph once again in season six? "It'll be interesting," Collins muses. "I think that the changes that have happened in his personality are gonna stick.

"I don't know what'll happen in season six, but my take is that he has to now have a more human personality. He has to have more empathy for humans. He's experienced too much of the human world now for it to not impact him in a big way. But his powers have been recharged, which is nice. He's kind of got the best of both worlds there."

CHUCK SHURLEY
This has been a really stressful day!

Chuck started season five with bits and pieces of Castiel stuck to him, which made coming back from the hiatus easy for Rob Benedict. "It's easy acting when you're covered in soot and fake bits of human flesh," he comments. "I'm like, 'Okay, I'm there. Roll the camera!' The prosthetic tooth that I had in my hair was pretty realistic and gooey. It was gross, but fun." Fun for the actor, but not so much for the character. "Chuck has a pretty shaky disposition as it is, so he's just barely keeping it together at that point. Chuck is in desperate need of therapy."

Fortunately, hanging out with the Winchester brothers has had a somewhat therapeutic effect on Chuck. "When Sam and Dean first found Chuck, he was a real recluse, he was drinking a lot and really down on himself," notes Benedict. "Then, through the course of the episodes, he found a renewed sense of something to care about. He cares about the guys and considers them almost his sons of sorts because he created them, so he feels a fatherly thing toward them... or maybe just a drunk uncle thing. So he gets energized and focused when it comes to trying to help them out."

Chuck also found someone new to care about in season five: Becky, his number one fan. Benedict thinks it's "awesome" that Chuck was given a love interest. "Emily Perkins is great, so that was super-fun," he says. "It was fun just to play that I had a thing for her when she was so not into me at first. Then I get to be the hero guy for a second." Benedict would like to play the hero more often too. "I love the action stuff, so I'd love for Chuck to go out on adventures with Sam and Dean." In that case, would Benedict start bodybuilding with Jared Padalecki and Jensen Ackles? "They have a gym trailer right on set that they can work out in during lunch, whereas I go and watch *Oprah*..."

Of course, after his mysterious vanishing act in 'Swan Song', will Chuck even be back in season six? "Anything could happen," Benedict teases. "I could never be seen again or be seen a lot. The way it's left at the end of the season, it could go either way."

Okay, but is Chuck God? "It's up in the air." 🖊

> **DID YOU KNOW?**
>
> Fans often ask Rob Benedict to write, "I am the Prophet Chuck," when he's signing autographs. "There are a lot of requests," he says, "like, 'draw a picture' or 'write on Dean's nose,' and other very specific things."

BOBBY SINGER

Brains trumps legs, apparently.

"**B**obby grew more depressed and cynical in season five as a result of his physical condition and loss of mobility and of the extremely dark future that seemed to lie ahead," notes Jim Beaver. "Bobby suffered more personally in this season than in any prior season, and we saw cracks begin to form in his tough exterior." Bobby's condition also affected his relationsh ip with Sam and Dean. "He became more and more dependent on them, and more emotionally isolated from them," Beaver feels. "They both moved to protect him as much as they could, but Bobby became more remote and less accepting of both their foibles and their care."

Unfortunately, Bobby's depression led to heavy drinking and talk of suicide. "I don't think Bobby was being melodramatic," Beaver contends, "but his actions speak louder than his words, as everyone's do. Bobby's actions have been to keep fighting. It doesn't mean he doesn't feel what he says he feels, but that ultimately he is what he does." So if he hadn't gotten his legs back in his deal with Crowley, he likely would have gone down fighting, running over monsters with his wheelchair right down to his last breath.

"I got to get up out of the chair whenever I wanted to, and I take that part of it very seriously," says Beaver, "but technically, filming in it was a little bit of a pain in the neck because it was harder to hit my mark, which I couldn't see as easily. There were cables and stuff that I had to roll over. I think I shared a little bit of Bobby's feelings, because it's not all that much fun to stay at home while the boys are out having adventures. They were pretty good about getting Bobby out of the house, but at the same time there were times when Bobby's at home and Jim's going, 'I'm just sitting here manning the phones and they're out there kicking ass!' That's no fun. On the other hand, dramatically, as an actor, I had a lot of really great emotional scenes to play as a result of being in the wheelchair."

Surprisingly, notorious pranksters Jared Padalecki and Jensen Ackles didn't take advantage of Beaver's limited mobility in season five. "They sometimes screw with my cues when it's my close-up, giving me different lines than are in the script to try to mess me up," he admits, "but there've been no big pranks. I'm tellin' ya, those boys are scared of me!"

Perhaps creator Eric Kripke's a little scared of Beaver, too. After all, it took him five seasons to get up the nerve to kill off Bobby, and then he brought him right back. Beaver certainly expects his character to last as long as the show does, no matter how long that is. "Sam and Dean will start to get old, but Bobby's perpetually young, so I'm not worried about him." ✐

DID YOU KNOW?

"Fans ask me to call them 'idjits' all the time," Jim Beaver shares.

NICK / LUCIFER

Oh, *hello*, Death.

When Mark Pellegrino was young, he never dreamed he would get to play the ultimate villain someday. "Not at all," he says. "In fact, when I was a kid, acting was the furthest thing from my mind. I was going to be a marine biologist until I was about nineteen." Even as an actor, he didn't have to dream about getting such a juicy role — it was handed to him. "I don't know what their thoughts were," he comments, regarding the executive producers choosing him to play Lucifer, "but I didn't audition."

He also didn't find it hard to step into the Devil's shoes. "I come from a broken home," Pellegrino reveals. "Lucifer did too, so I didn't have to dig too deep to find that grief." Another key to making Lucifer real for him was, "Understanding Lucifer not as some celestial being that I can't identify with, but as a person who has a real bone to pick with his family. He feels he was betrayed by his father and brother for people he thinks are less worthy than him, and he wants revenge. I think anybody can relate to that; it's a very simple human issue.

"The fact that Lucifer told the truth is an interesting irony, seeing as how he's the Prince of Lies in our mythology. That actually helps me to empathize with the character and get on my own side, so to speak. I don't think as an actor you should say, 'I'm playing the jerk' or 'the bad guy.' You have to be on your own side. Lucifer tells the truth and has some valid criticisms that make sense to a guy like Nick, who's lost everything, so I had a very strong emotional base to work from."

Despite the darkness that surrounds a character like Lucifer, Pellegrino still enjoyed playing the part. "The easiest part was, believe it or not, that it needed to be fun," he states. "I think Lucifer is an interesting character because he's funny, and I got to be playful with the role."

While he enjoyed playing Lucifer as an empathetic fallen angel, Pellegrino was really excited to finally show Lucifer's true colors — and immense powers — in 'Hammer of the Gods'. "Pretty much the whole time, getting revenge for his betrayal is his mission," Pellegrino points out, "but what changed about him then was that he went from a rather docile guy who relied on the strength of his argument to somebody who kicked some ass, which I think is great. He dealt a little punishment to the pagan upstarts who thought they could stand in his way. I loved that!"

The Nick meatsuit was always meant as a temporary vessel for Lucifer, though, and the fallen angel's jump to Sam's body signaled the end of Pellegrino's run on *Supernatural*. "I really liked being on the show," he says. "I'm hoping they'll find a way to keep Nick's vessel somehow minimally alive — on life-support."

DID YOU KNOW?

When Mark Pellegrino was a kid, he wore a plastic Devil mask for Halloween. "I couldn't see very well," he recalls. "I ran into the door of one of the houses I was trick-or-treating at and smashed the entire front of the mask, so maybe somebody was telling me something."

ELLEN HARVELLE

You can go straight back to Hell, you ugly bitch!

After a memorable run of episodes in season two, Samantha Ferris had expected her character, hunter Ellen Harvelle, who was also somewhat of a surrogate mother for the Winchester boys, to return in season three. However, the writers weren't able to work Ellen into the season's storylines until the last episode, and then the producers were unable to book Ferris. "I just couldn't do it," she recalls. "So I was like, 'Okay, that's over.' Then I get a phone call two years later..."

Ellen returned as if she had never left, simply admonishing Dean for not keeping in touch. "I played her the same way," Ferris says. "She was a great character, tough as nails, so I think changing her would've been a mistake." The only difference was in her relationship with her daughter, Jo, who she treated with the respect a fellow hunter deserves. "In those couple of years, Jo went out hunting by herself and managed to stay alive. I'll always see her as my daughter, but I respected her more as an equal."

Ferris figured the Harvelles would be killed off in 'Good God Y'all', so when they weren't, she thought, "'Okay, we're in the clear.' Then, sure enough, I got a call from executive producer Phil Sgriccia. He said, 'There's good news and bad news.' I'm like, 'Oh, I know the bad news — *we're dying.*' He said, 'But you guys go out in a blaze of glory — you're taking the big one for the team.' So I'm like, 'Okay, I can't complain about that.' It was very heroic, and Alona and I gave it everything we had. It was our last scene, so there were some natural emotions going on there. I got about two hundred messages from fans saying how moved they were by that final scene. The great thing about that scene is you got to see the tough broad that everybody related to, but you also got to see her be a mom and be vulnerable at the end of her life."

Of course, the end of her life doesn't necessarily mean it's the end of Ellen on *Supernatural*. "I emailed Eric Kripke and thanked him for everything," says Ferris, "and he sent a very nice email back, saying, 'Death means nothing on this show. Don't get too excited. You're not gone yet.' I'd really like to come back, even if it's just one episode toward the very end." ✐

JO HARVELLE

This is why we're here, right? If I could get us a shot at the Devil...

"I had no expectations that I'd be back," Alona Tal admits, so she was ecstatic when she got the call to return. But she was a little nervous when she arrived at the set. "It's kind of like going back to school after you've already graduated," she relates. "I was excited, but I was like, 'I hope it goes well.'"

Most of the crew hadn't changed, so it was like a homecoming for the actress, but her character *had* changed significantly. "I think we're kind of reflected in our characters," she says. "I've grown up in the last few years, so I think Jo grew up a lot, too. I really wanted to make her not be as extroverted. Before, she was very quick on the trigger, verbally — quick to have a smartass comeback — and I didn't want that this time. I wanted to play her more centered. The best part was that I got to have more action and enjoy the benefit of the doubt with her because having a competent character is always fun."

Jo was still at odds with her mother, Ellen, when they returned in 'Good God, Y'all', only instead of them fighting about whether Jo should be hunting, they were hunting each other, both believing the other was a demon. Jo even called her mom an evil skank! "That was so weird," Tal exclaims. "I don't call people that. I don't use words like skank, I just don't. Having to say that was very challenging, because I had to mean it whole-heartedly, so it was funny. Every time I said that, Sam Ferris and I laughed. But I got to have a little fight with my mom, which was fun. I hurt myself filming that scene. Just some bruises and a bump on my arm, though, nothing crazy."

Nothing as crazy as getting your guts clawed out by a hellhound? "Oh, that was a lot of fun! I got to have a prosthetic of my stomach being ripped open." Tal's family didn't find anything fun about her onscreen death, however. "It was horrific for my family," she says. "My mother started to watch it and stopped. She was like, 'I can't.' My sister had nightmares.

"I was bummed out that they killed Jo off," Tal concludes, "but it was a very heroic death, and you can't ask for anything better."

DID YOU KNOW?

Alona Tal celebrated her birthday on the set of 'Abandon All Hope'. "We were shooting in the hardware store that day," she recalls, "so everyone just grabbed the most random thing — like nails and duct tape — and gave it to me. 'Here! Happy birthday!' It was silly but fun."

ADAM MILLIGAN / MICHAEL

Oh, me and some archangel are gonna kill the Devil.

"I'm bad about watching TV," Jake Abel admits, "so I never really caught *Supernatural* before I was on it. But I have friends who are big fans, and they were really excited when I got the part." His friends warned him about how loyal the fans are to Sam and Dean too, so, "It was terrifying," he says. "The idea of a third brother pissed a lot of people off. But I think the payoff in 'Jump the Shark' helped a lot, and the fans accepted me."

The payoff being that the real Adam was already dead, with his body all eaten up. "I thought that was great!" Abel enthuses. "My mom hated it. She said that's something a mother never wants to see." Mothers would probably prefer not to see their sons transformed into bloodthirsty ghouls, either. "Yeah, but that was fun," says Abel. "My favorite part was when Jared Padalecki was all tied up and I was slamming the knife by his head. That wasn't in the script, and Jared didn't know I was gonna do it. After a couple of takes I was like, 'Are you okay with this?' and he said, 'If it looks good, just do it — but don't hit me.' I was like, 'Alright!'"

Even though he enjoyed playing the ghoul, Abel was happy to show viewers what the real Adam is like. "The ghoul had Adam's memories, but he didn't really know how Adam would act, which is why he's so whiny and all that. In 'Point of No Return' we found that the real Adam is a lot like Dean; a little cynical and a real smartass. So I really tried to get that Winchester family thing going. My character didn't grow up with them, but there's some nature versus nurture, so I figured my voice and a few body tics should be similar to Sam and Dean, and John, too."

When Adam then became Archangel Michael's meatsuit, Abel says, "I was trying to be epic with my portrayal of Michael. There were these giant turbines blowing wind, and I had this badass power stance and Jared across from me as Lucifer. I just got a feel for the character and I rolled with it. It was a blast. I really had a great experience the entire time on *Supernatural*." ✦

DID YOU KNOW?

Jake Abel co-starred with Ted Raimi of 'Wishful Thinking' fame in *Angel of Death*, but contrary to what the title suggests, the movie features an assassin rather than a murderous supernatural angel.

ZACHARIAH

In Heaven I have six wings and four faces, one of which is a lion.

"The thing that I love about *Supernatural* and playing Zachariah," says Kurt Fuller, "is the themes are huge and mythic. You don't just get angry, you get *furious*. If you're upset, you don't just slap somebody in the face, you *take away their lungs*! That kind of stuff is fantastic to play. Maybe it's because I'm a big ham, but it's the greatest of all jobs."

Yet even taking Sam's lungs away didn't get Dean to give in to Zachariah's demands. "I thought Dean was going to be easy," Fuller says. "I thought he was just a loser without much backbone, but he had more backbone and was brighter than I had any idea he was going to be. Then instead of that making me respect him more, it makes me despise him more, because he really is in my way. I have one thing I have to do. *One thing!* I have to get Dean to say yes to Michael. If he says yes, I'm moving up a level, getting a big promotion. But this filthy, smelly little thing, this inferior incarnation of life, this *human*, won't say it, no matter what I do."

Still, Zachariah torturing Sam and Dean to get Dean to become Michael's vessel could be justifiable in a the-end-justifies-the-means sense, but in 'Point of No Return' he tortures Adam just for the pleasure of it. "When I first took the role, I thought Zachariah was going to be a benign sort of guiding hand," Fuller admits. "It really surprised me when he turned as dark as he did. But in 'Dark Side of the Moon', Zachariah says, 'It's personal now, boys.' So by 'Point of No Return', Zachariah has really cracked. He's fifty-two percent revenge, forty-eight percent still trying to make his plan work."

Thing is, "Zachariah views himself as a great guy," Fuller points out. "He views himself as the only one who knows what is really going on. He's the only one who actually has a plan to defeat Lucifer that's going to work. If only people would listen to him!"

Fortunately, his plan didn't work. Unfortunately, yet another great character was killed off the show. "The nature of the job is to become emotionally connected, so when you get killed it's no fun," says Fuller. "I was actually very upset that he was dying, because it honestly was a part of me that died."

YOUNG JOHN WINCHESTER

You all mighta treated me like a fool, but I am not *useless*.

"I was lucky enough to have a somewhat similar look to Jeffrey Dean Morgan," points out Matt Cohen, discussing his audition for Young John Winchester. "I have a good relationship with casting director Robert Ulrich, so as long as my acting could pull it off, I kinda felt like I had it in the bag, and that was that. It was really exciting to get to play a character established by an actor I admire. I think Jeffrey is a brilliant actor. I would love to meet him and work with him one day.

"I was more than excited to get the chance to come back to *Supernatural*, especially to play Young John Winchester. He's just a good, wholesome character, and the fact that I got to play in the seventies time era made me feel lucky for that reason as well." Of course, Cohen hadn't even been born in the seventies. "My dad was around twenty years old during that time period, and I've seen lots of things from when he was younger, so I pulled from that a lot," the actor notes. "I watched whatever I could on Jeffrey, too, including other characters outside of his John Winchester; just anything I could pull from him and date a little bit. I kinda just morphed it all into something that I prayed would work."

On top of that, Cohen had a little help from a new friend. "Jensen Ackles took me aside and gave me some behind-the-scenes details about things that had happened in previous episodes with character development and things like that that I could bring to my character." Cohen further describes the personality of the character he brought to life. "Young John's this all-American, golden-hearted, Mr. Do-Right guy. He cares about the right things and doesn't want to do the wrong thing. He has a stern presence, but there's a giant teddy bear heart behind that front. He's protective. To describe him in brief, I'd say he wants what's right and he wants to give what's expected of him all the time without fail."

Cohen would definitely return to *Supernatural* again without fail. "They all just made me feel right at home," he says. "I felt like I was a series regular and I'd worked with these guys all my life. Literally everybody from craft services to the executive producers is a ten on that set." ✐

DID YOU KNOW?

Matt Cohen starred in *Boogeyman 2*, the sequel to *Supernatural* creator Eric Kripke's feature film screenwriting début, *Boogeyman*.

YOUNG MARY WINCHESTER

Last time I saw you, a demon *killed* my *parents.*

"I definitely think my resemblance to Samantha Smith helped get me the audition," notes Amy Gumenick. "I remember walking into the initial audition, and I was a little intimidated by how many girls looked like me — it was a room full of petite, blonde, blue-eyed girls. It was funny. During the audition, they had a picture of Samantha Smith blown up, and as I was reading the casting director would look back and forth between me and her picture." After she got the role, Gumenick looked to Smith for comparison as well. "I watched as much of Sam's performances of Mary as I could get my hands on. More than anything I wanted to capture the essence of Mary, but also I think that, as people, Sam and I have a lot of similar mannerisms. I think our similarities were just innately there, but I definitely watched for small subtleties and tried to incorporate those in my portrayal of Mary.

"Something that I found interesting was playing a role that was already so established and loved," Gumenick says. "It's a little bit scary, because the fans are expecting a lot, so when I got to set, one of the first things the director said to me was, 'I want you to create your own Mary.' The younger Mary and older Mary are at such different places in their lives, they are essentially different people. So the Mary I created has more of a feistiness about her; she's a little bit rebellious and a little bit resentful about the life that she's been forced into living. The best way I can describe her is that she's a free spirit who wants to go out and have fun and be normal and have friends and a relationship with John. There's a constant struggle and a lot of pain surrounding the fact that she has to live this double life. It's a really interesting internal struggle for her, I think. More than anything, she really wants to share that life with John, but is scared."

Gumenick, on the other hand, is happy to share in the world of *Supernatural*, and is looking forward to the writers finding a way to bring her back in season six. "When I went back to do 'The Song Remains the Same', I felt like I was going back to play with my friends. It was great." ✍

CROWLEY

They ate my tailor.

"Crowley is an awful lot of fun to play," states Mark Sheppard. "I'm so proud that the character has resonated with the fans. It's been wonderful."

Sheppard shares his perspective on what he feels are "the two great types of characters to play. You either want to play the last sane man in the universe or you want to play the guy that sold him out before he left the planet. Those are the two guys. The first one is Eddie Albert's Oliver Wendell Douglas on *Green Acres*. The other one is Dr. Zachary Smith from *Lost in Space*. I think Crowley is very much the last sane man in the universe. I find him very similar to Romo Lampkin [of *Batttlestar Galactica*] in a way. He has a very different personality, but his fundamental beliefs, his wants and his desires, are as altruistic as any other of those types of characters that I've played."

One can't help but wonder if Sheppard is drawn to those types of characters because of similarities to his own personality. "I guess some things might be a facet of me," he acquiesces. "I have no idea. But I love the idea of a man with a plan. It's always better than trying to play evil, which gives you nowhere to go — if I'm just bad, I'm vastly uninteresting. You definitely get the feeling that Crowley has a plan."

So far that plan has involved giving Sam and Dean the Colt, helping locate Pestilence and Death, and borrowing Bobby's soul. Does he have anything else in mind for the Winchesters? "It's fascinating to me that Sam and Dean are very different around Crowley than they are around anyone else," notes Sheppard. "I think they treat Crowley completely differently than anyone else that I've seen. He's quite abusive to them at times, and they kind of skip over that. Maybe they accept that as part of his nature. Or maybe it's because the things that Crowley does tend to be of some importance.

"With the jeopardy of the Apocalypse removed, it should be interesting to see how their treatment of Crowley is next season," Sheppard muses. "I mean, are they going to be adversaries of Crowley's? Are they going to team up with him? Is Crowley gonna hand Bobby's soul back? If so, what about the legs? Crowley's not the easiest person to have hanging around." ✍

THE TRICKSTER / LOKI / GABRIEL

I wish this were a TV show. Easy answers, endings wrapped up in a bow. But this is real. And it's gonna end bloody for all of us.

Richard Speight Jr. was hoping to get a call to play the Trickster in season four, but when that didn't happen, he thought, "That ship has sailed," so he was "surprised to get the call in season five." He even received a promotion of sorts, going from monster-of-the-week to a key figure in the show's mythos. "That was a nice bolster to the ego," he agrees. "I didn't see that coming! I loved the character anyway, but for them to give the character more importance in the overall story is awesome."

Even though Sam and Dean discovered that the Trickster was actually Archangel Gabriel, they weren't able to convince him to help stop the Apocalypse, at least not at first. "At the end of 'Changing Channels', he comes out with his whole philosophy," Speight says, "which is, 'I don't want to get involved in this. I know what's going to happen, but I'm not going to intercede. I'm just gonna wait on the sidelines, and I want you guys to shut up and do all the heavy lifting.' Dean calls him out on how he is afraid of his family, and I think it leaves Gabriel with a lot on his mind as far as what his role should be."

Likewise, Speight had a lot on his mind after reading the script for 'Hammer of the Gods'. "There's the Richard Speight-as-an-actor reaction," he says, "which is, 'Oh, crap, I'm dead!' It's my favorite character I've ever gotten to play on TV. It's so much fun, and there are so many layers to it. So for that reason I was disappointed. But as far as where I saw Gabriel's involvement in the show going, I was thrilled, because I'd always wanted Gabriel to reveal himself to be on the boys' side. I'd always thought he had a strong affection for the Winchester brothers, that there was something in their fraternal bond and his lack thereof that he found intriguing and admired about them. So if he was going to get involved in the Apocalypse, I wanted him to be on what I thought was the right side. Obviously I don't get a say in the matter, but I'm glad the writers saw it the same way. To see that when the defecation's about to hit the oscillation he makes the right decision, that was really important to me." ✎

DID YOU KNOW?

"I figure Gabriel has his own space upstairs where he messes with people on the wrong side of his fight," says Richard Speight Jr., speculating on where Gabriel sent Castiel in 'Changing Channels', "like that bad neighbor kid in *Toy Story* who has the creepy room and messes with all the toys."

MEG

Lucifer's gonna take over Heaven.

Rachel Miner hadn't watched *Supernatural* prior to landing the role of Meg — a reprise of the demon character formerly embodied by Nicki Aycox — so right before she left for Vancouver she watched a clip of one of Aycox's performances online. "I wanted to make sure I wasn't doing anything too far from what she'd done," says Miner. "It was interesting to me, because Meg is written so specifically that the choices were very similar. I didn't have to shift anything about my performance, really — it was serendipitous. Meg is such a free spirit that I wanted to let some of that come across, too."

Miner sums up her character in one word: "Fiery. There's just this devilish enjoyment that she gets out of playing cat-and-mouse with the boys. She's lived for thousands of years, and she's had so much experience that I think the little things wouldn't be significant to her, so there's a sense of fun about her, even though she's obviously very evil, and what she finds fun is twisted.

"She likes toying with the boys," Miner says. "Like when I got to hold Sam and tease him a little bit and say, 'Not so easy without those super-special demon powers, huh, Sammy?' I just loved saying, 'I always knew you were a big, dumb, slow, pain in the ass, Dean.' So much fun!"

Part of the evil fun of being a demon is hopping from body to body, yet Miner wasn't worried when the demon smoked out of her meatsuit at the end of 'Sympathy for the Devil'. "I'd been told they'd bring me back, so I had my fingers crossed," she explains. "It was funny, because I'd gotten an offer for a film and made my managers hold out until I found out if they wanted to bring me back on *Supernatural* during that time period. I had my managers call and luckily they said, 'Yes, we do want to bring her back for that time,' so I turned down the film."

Miner is looking forward to the chance to make *Supernatural* her top choice again in season six. "I'm pretty sure that I'm not dead, so I'll wait and see," she says. "I really hope they bring me back, because the character's so much fun and the people are so amazing to work with, and the fans are so loving." ✐

DID YOU KNOW?

"I really loved getting to kick Jared Padalecki's butt in 'Sympathy for the Devil'," shares Rachel Miner. "He's quite big and muscular, so getting to take him down was fun!"

MEET THE CREW: GRAPHIC DESIGN

"Typically, on a TV show, or even on a feature film, there is only one graphic artist," points out graphic artist Lee Anne Elaschuk. "However, *Supernatural* requires two because of the sheer volume of graphics that we have to generate. Every time Sam and Dean pick up a book, pick up a beer, walk down a street, anything they do usually involves some sort of graphics that we need to create. The other thing about this show is that we move to a different location every single episode and we don't have any standing sets, so we have to reinvent Vancouver to look like somewhere in the U.S. every episode, and we try to do that as best we can. For instance, we'll go to that city's Chamber of Commerce website for research. We get as detailed as we can so that we can incorporate those elements into our graphics. We do all the signs and everything that help make a place look like where it's supposed to be."

"I love to do the little stuff and especially put some humor in it," says Elaschuk. "One time, I was doing some menu cards for a restaurant, and Eggs Benedict was not in the spellchecker, so it was trying to replace Benedict with bandicoot and bayonet and all these hilarious words, so I made each menu say something different. There was Eggs Bandicoot, Eggs Bayonet, Eggs Bonjour, anything that spellcheck replaced it with, I made one like that. So our extras, who were sitting at the tables, might have had one that said something really bizarre.

"Sometimes we'll put people's names in the menus, like Bob's chilli or whatever," she adds. "I don't use my own name that much," comments graphic designer Mary-Ann Liu, but I've been a doctor, an author, you name it. Some people will say, 'I want to be this.' Some people go, 'No, not on a tombstone.' 'No, you can't put my kid on a missing poster.' I totally understand that and am respectful of that. There are a few people who'll say, 'Hey, you haven't used my name in a while,' but you can't use any name too often or

Left
Design for the magic shop sign in 'I Believe the Children Are Our Future'.

Above Left

Jacket art for the book that Sheriff Mills reads to her son in 'Dead Men Don't Wear Plaid'.

Above Right

The "thirties glamour Hollywood" painting from 'Monster Movie'.

else it becomes too obvious." They can't use any name without clearance from the legal department either. "It's site specific," Liu explains. "Let's say we're in Wisconsin, then they'll actually look up the name in the city and make sure there's no conflict."

Whether an episode is set in Wisconsin or any other American locale, the show is known for its motels, and the graphic designers definitely enjoy working on them. "A few seasons ago I came up with the first tent card, and it was a really simple one," recalls Liu. "Lee Anne took that concept and ran with it for the next episode and developed the fancier tent card. Then we started to make them more and more special, and the directors picked up on that and started using them as a reveal. So now there are always those extra little bits in the motel rooms. A fun tent card I did was the one that tells you about the Casa Erotica adult channel for the Elysian Fields Hotel in 'Hammer of the Gods'. I used metal vinyl, and it looked very 3D. That one was a lot of work because we produce the tent cards by hand since there's usually only three or four of them.

"Another really fun thing to do was the picture of the female star for Dracula's dungeon in [season four's] 'Monster Movie'," says Liu. "The actress, Holly Dignard, gave us a picture with no makeup or anything, and my job was to turn that into a thirties glamour Hollywood picture, so I basically did a full makeup job on top of that."

That photo and the Casa Erotica tent card were topics of conversation in their episodes, but sometimes items the graphic designers labor on with love don't even make it into final cut. "That happens all the time," Liu confirms. "You don't know what the camera is going to see. You could be doing something in a book and it becomes an extreme close-up, so you have to prepare for any eventuality. You can't go, 'It's just a label,' because you don't know what the camera is going to see. There's no such thing as, 'Oh, I'll just do it quickly.' Everything we do, we do our best. That's our team.

"Everybody does their best to make the strongest design they can, and that's what gives our show a really cool edge," feels Liu. "We add little layers to the story, and we get a kick out of what we do." ✍

MEET THE CREW:
POST PRODUCTION

Producer Todd Aronauer works in post-production, where he deals with "the schedules, budgets, visual effects, audio, and everything they shoot in Vancouver. Anything that's playback and anything that's music-oriented comes through my department," he explains. "Then we take all the pieces of the puzzle and put them together in a nice, finalized package. We deal with all the cuts that each episode goes through."

"It's a great show to work on," Aronauer enthuses. "I'm glad it's lasted this long." Even after five seasons, his job is never dull. "Every episode is different from any we've done before, and every episode has its own obstacles, where any little thing can trip you up or slip through the cracks, so it's a challenging show in that respect because there are so many elements on any given episode that need to come together. It's a lot of fun when you've been working on the same show for five seasons and you're still able to do new things and it still makes you laugh. I can't tell you how many times I watch any given episode before we deliver it, so if I'm still laughing in the right places, that's a good thing."

One of the episodes that made Aronauer laugh a lot was season three's 'Ghostfacers', including the behind-the-scenes decision-making process that went into the bleeping out of unacceptable words. "In our rough cut, we weren't bleeping out enough according to Standards and Practices," shares Aronauer. "It's interesting to see the list of things the actors can't say. We thought about just putting in bleeps over words that didn't need to be bleeped, since the unnecessary censorship would've been funny, but we ended up just bleeping out what we were required to. We're always surprised by things that Standards and Practices force us to bleep out, cover up, shorten, or blur," he adds. "Though I think we're more surprised by what they say is okay. Like, you can't say, 'Jesus!' but you can say, 'bitch.' Then we see a note saying, 'I can see this person's butt crack, can you fuzz it out?' We show a lot of blood and guts, but they let that stuff past."

It's a good thing they let the blood past, otherwise the season five title card wouldn't be so visceral. When creating the title cards, Aronauer says, "We're always trying to figure out what's gonna look cool and what direction the season is going in, because we always want to add some sort of link to what we're going to see in the

Below

Motel tent card from
'My Bloody Valentine'.

season coming up. The season five blood theme has to do with the Winchester bloodline and also with Sam drinking blood. We tried a whole bunch of things and that was the one that we really felt captured the arc of what we were doing. It just gave the creepiest effect to everybody when they saw it."

Aronauer likes working for a show that has a creepy effect on people. "I enjoy hearing from people that the show is too scary to watch," he admits. "I'd rather they watch it, but if they're scared then we're doing what we set out to do."

It's associate producer Kristin Cronin's job to make sure that everything the producers set out to do gets done before the show hits the air. "I'm in charge of making sure that 'final texture' for the show, like the visual effects, color, and everything, is what Eric Kripke, Bob Singer, Phil Sgriccia, and Todd want," she explains. "I'm pretty much the last one to watch, " he admits. "I'd rather they watch it, but if they're scared then we're doing what we set out to do."

It's associate producer Kristin Cronin's job to make sure that everything the producers set out to do gets done before the show hits the air. "I'm in charge of making sure that 'final texture' for the show, like the visual effects, color, and everything, is what Eric Kripke, Bob Singer, Phil Sgriccia, and Todd want," she explains. "I'm pretty much the last one to watch the show before it's delivered to The CW.

"When we do week-of mixes for the show, which is whenever production catches up with post-production, delivery can be two days before it airs," she reveals. "That's unavoidable when you're getting last-minute effects. Visual effects are heavy on this show, and some of our episodes have so many amazing effects that they take as long as possible to get them as perfect as they can before it airs." Getting episodes out with no time to spare would seem like a high stress job, but Cronin says, "I've been doing it for five years, so it's not as bad as you would think. Everything runs so well, we all know each other and what has to happen, and we've been through so many different situations together."

The systems they have in place run so smoothly, in fact, that Cronin could not think of any significant challenges in recent memory. "Everything is completely mathematical," she says. "We tell the visual effects department exactly how much we need, to the frame. We have everything exactly as we need it or the show wouldn't come together and we'd have to redo a lot of stuff. And that's never happened." 🖉

DO YOU BELIEVE?
YOUNG JOHN WINCHESTER: Monsters are real.

Do *you* believe in the supernatural?

"I definitely do," says Cindy Sampson. "They're watching us! Those moments where you get the creeps, like when your hair stands up on end on the back of your neck? Anyone who doesn't have that in their life may just be fooling themselves."

Amy Gumenick has that in her life, but she wishes she didn't. "I like to pretend that it's not real," she says, "because of my imagination — I create some good horror for myself. I get affected by ghost stories and supernatural occurrences that people talk about. Luckily I haven't had any encounters myself, but I believe it's out there."

Gumenick's onscreen husband, Matt Cohen, hasn't had any encounters either, but he says, "I do have feelings sometimes that things have happened, that strange presences are by me, so I can't say I don't believe. I think that it's a little naïve to think that we are the only things that are here. I'm not super-religious, but I believe there's a Heaven, an afterlife. I believe there's a better place when you've gone. You have to believe that, right? You can't live every day thinking, 'Oh, there's just nothing.' You've always got to stay on the positive side, put out that good energy, and hopefully that's returned to you."

Mark Pellegrino also hopes there's a Heaven, and the onscreen Devil hopes there's a Hell, too. "I hope the people that do horrible things to other human beings here and get away with it all through their lives or get off with easy punishments will somehow feel what they've done in the other realm and pay for it in some way." Pellegrino has reason to believe that other realms exist. "I had some experiences after my mom died where I was reconnecting with her," he shares. "I was reconnecting with her on a different plane — literally not in this world, but somewhere else. There was a glow to her and a happiness to her that was very otherworldly. There was knowledge and wisdom in her face that was very striking to me."

It seems as if Pellegrino might have been having an out-of-body experience when he reconnected with his mother. Mary-Ann Liu recounts her own ethereal experience. "I've had one out-of-body experience," she declares. "I was a teenager and I saw a symbol on the wall in my room — which I could draw for you right now, it's still that clear — and I knew the symbol wasn't actually on the wall. I felt myself sinking in and then I lifted and turned around and saw myself. I freaked out and sort of jumped back in."

Maybe Kristin Cronin has encountered astral projections of live people such as Liu, since she says, "I've gotten feelings that 'something' was out there, but I don't know about things like vampires and werewolves."

Above

Sam and Dean find themselves in Heaven in 'Dark Side of the Moon'.

Of course, those things could just be good old-fashioned ghosts, which Chad Lindberg regularly encounters. "I've seen many," he states. "Last good one I can remember, I was with a friend out at 3:30 in the morning, and we were standing on a sidewalk and we saw this woman walk across the block in this black evening gown. We couldn't see her face because she was halfway up the block. She was bending down and picking up these big long pieces of grass. She had her left arm out like she was cradling a baby, and she was laying these flowers really slowly and methodically into her hand. We thought it was weird, so we walked toward her to get a better look at her, but she started walking away from us. We got right up behind her and realized we couldn't hear her walking. We went around her to check out her face, but she wouldn't let us see her face. The way she did it was the creepiest thing ever. Then she sat down on the curb, still hiding her face, and we kept walking because we didn't want to scare her. After ten or fifteen feet, we turned to each other and were like, 'You know what? I think that was a ghost!' We walked back two seconds later and she was gone. Then later I found out that a lady had died there. So that was an interesting experience."

"My wife has a friend who actually lives in a haunted house," states David Reed. "Her friend's grandmother is in a wheelchair, and one day the family heard noises up in the attic of this house. My wife's friend and her parents went up to the attic to see what the noise was, and they couldn't find anything. They were like, 'Oh, it must have been a box falling or something.' Then they turned around and there's Grandma — she couldn't walk, but she was standing there — and she said, 'They want us to leave.' I don't know what happened after that."

Maybe the ghosts tracked Reed through his wife and followed him to work, which would explain the odd experiences he's had in the *Supernatural* offices. "We're

in a different building than we were in last season, and right outside the door of my office there is this set of fluorescent lights, and right when we moved in they started flickering a lot, all the time, and making funny noises, like electric feedback noises," he says. "I would stand by it and it was really, really cold in that spot. Perhaps because of the air-conditioning vent over it, but more likely because we have ghosts in the building. I'm pretty sure, but they haven't caused any problems — *yet*."

If the ghosts do cause any problems, Reed could always call in Rachel Minor for help. "I haven't had anything happen like what the boys have experienced on the show," she says, "but if that happened I would take them on!" In fact, Miner might have already had some close brushes with supernatural creatures, so perhaps they have just chosen to steer clear of her, sensing the hunter inside her. "I've definitely had some interesting experiences," she says. "Certainly in older buildings and stuff, but I don't quite know exactly if I should explain that. Let's just say I'm open to a lot of things."

Mark Sheppard is likewise open to just about anything. "I think it would be ridiculous to not believe that there are things outside our knowledge, understanding, and experience," he says. "I think it would be very narrow-minded to think that what we see and know is everything. Of course there are things that we can't fathom or understand! I've had several experiences with things I couldn't fathom — some of them on the set of *Supernatural*, actually." It seems, however, that his strange encounters spooked him into silence, since Sheppard refuses to elaborate on his experiences, saying only, "Well, that would be telling." But he put things in perspective for all of us by concluding: "Are there not some things in everyone's life that you just really cannot explain?" ✐

SUPERNATURAL REACTION

"... this series has topped itself every season..."
— Robert Philpot, *Fort Worth Star-Telegram*

According to *TV Guide*, *Supernatural* has "only gotten better with age." Echoing the sentiment, Ed Martin of the *Huffington Post* says *Supernatural* "has evolved into one of the best shows on television, period." Maureen Ryan of the *Chicago Tribune* praises *Supernatural* for being "consistently satisfying." The show's quality is also regularly recognized. *Supernatural* was number one on *iF Magazine*'s Best TV Shows of 2009 list, it won the Best TV Show title in the *SFX Magazine* Awards, it was the People's Choice Awards 2010 winner for Best Sci-Fi/Fantasy Show, and *Entertainment Weekly* named it as one of the 25 Greatest Cult TV Shows Ever.

"It's really cool," Jensen Ackles says, regarding the show's cult popularity. "I've had everything from the valet guy going, 'Hey, man, I love your show,' to a hyperventilating teenager coming up and wanting me to sign something, so it's really unique. It's definitely an experience I cherish." Rob Benedict likewise finds the fan reaction "touching. I'm blown away by the life *Supernatural* has beyond the TV screen," he says. "I've rarely seen this kind of fandom and devotion. I love it."

Supernatural fans are very active online, and in anticipation of the season five premiere, they started ending their Twitter posts with the tag "luciferiscoming," which reached the top position on the site's trending charts. Then a certain entertainer, unaware of the context of luciferiscoming, and perhaps thinking Satanists were involved, started a new trend tagged with "godishere." Before things turned into a full-on religious war and got out of hand, Twitter blocked posts with God and Lucifer tags from appearing on the trending lists. So *Supernatural* fans continued to hype the season five premiere with tags such as "supernatural" and "inkripkewetrust," and Misha Collins got into the fun with the tag, "pdiddyisscaredofhistv."

Fans in the U.K. got to go beyond the online environs to help promote the season five premiere on Living TV. The network ran a reality game called "Fight the Apocalypse," which was based at the website www.luciferiscoming.com. Players had to find Enochian sigils that were hidden both online and in real world locations throughout the U.K.

Fans around the world can now get into the hunt anytime they want as Margaret Weis Productions has released the long-awaited *Supernatural* Role Playing Game. There are also two more books in the RPG series — *Adventures*, and the *Guide to the Hunted* — as well as a free beginner's guide, *The Hunt Begins* (available from DriveThru RPG).

Fans would do well not to miss any story that comes out of the *Supernatural* universe by picking up copies of all the officially licensed novels and comics. Author Keith R.A. DeCandido, who has already established his great grasp of the show's characters in *Nevermore* and *Bone Key*, returns with *Heart of the Dragon*, wherein he brings John Winchester and the Campbells (Mary, Samuel, and Deanna) to life in a story that pits Sam and Dean against a monster that their parents and grandparents failed to defeat. New to the *Supernatural* universe is author Joe Schreiber, whose *The Unholy Cause* drops the brothers and Castiel into the middle of a Civil War re-enactment overrun by demons connected to the legendary Judas Iscariot. Rounding off the recent batch of novels is *War of the Sons* by Rebecca Dessertine, co-writer of the *Supernatural* comic series *Rising Son* and assistant to Eric Kripke, and David Reed, *Supernatural*'s script coordinator. Their story sends Sam and Dean back to the 1950s, though Reed would have been happy writing about the boys in any time period. "The best part was getting to write Dean cracking wise," he says. "It's really easy picturing Jensen Ackles being funny, and it's easy for me to picture Sam being stoic and furrowing his brow."

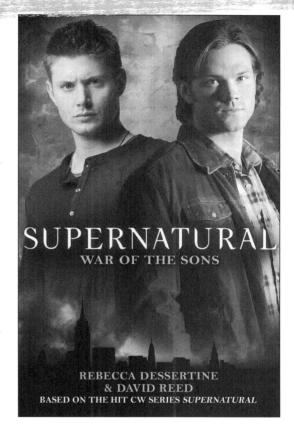

Above
Cover art for the sixth *Supernatural* tie-in novel, *War of the Sons*.

"Sam is so serious," agrees staff writer Daniel Loflin, who co-wrote the third *Supernatural* comic series, *Beginning's End*, with his screenwriting partner, Andrew Dabb. "That's one of the things we tried to tackle with the comic books: 'Why is Sam so serious?' It's basically because before Mary died, Dean got to experience life with her and with John as a normal dad, whereas Sam grew up with this hardened, militaristic, revenge-driven man, so Sam reflects the serious side of John Winchester and Dean the more carefree side."

Of course, anytime you need a fix of Sam and Dean Winchester, there is always the season five DVD set, which has an unaired scene from 'The Real Ghostbusters', commentary for 'The End', the always much-anticipated gag reel, Bobby's Apocalypse Survival Guides, and the Ghostfacers web series.

In case you actually need any encouragement to purchase the DVDs or tune in next season, Matt Rousch of *TV Guide* sums the show up nicely: "At its entertaining best, *Supernatural* is a ridiculously scary, frighteningly funny thrill ride with a fiercely emotional center." ✑

SURVIVING THE APOCALYPSE

If the Apocalypse were to arrive for real tomorrow, would you be prepared? "Not at all," Eric Kripke declares. "It's the *Apocalypse* and I'm just a writer, so I think I would quickly soil my pants. Then, if I had the ability to pull myself together, I would spend time with my family until lights out."

"Just get your family close and find a good hiding place," agrees Rob Benedict, "and, of course, horde toilet paper. Every once in a while I think, 'Maybe I'll put some more water in the garage. Although I don't know how that's going to help me if something crushes my house." Misha Collins doesn't have an answer for him. "I'm not one of those people who saves potatoes and fresh water and duct tape in the trunk of my car," he says. "I probably would be thoroughly unprepared for any kind of apocalypse."

"I don't think I would be prepared," admits Alona Tal. "That's a very deep question, especially since a lot of people believe it is coming. I think that if you look at the rules of human conduct, you just have to follow basic moral codes. I try to follow them as best as possible. I try to be a good person, and I think that if this were to happen, I would be within that moral code and would know what to do."

Charlie Crutcher shares Tal's belief that being a good person now is what will save him in the end. "You have to remember that this is not a practice life and that it could be over tomorrow," he says. "Basically, be thankful for what you have and help out the guy on the street and the man on the corner, because you never know who they might be. In the show you never know who is who, and it's the same thing in real life. Think about it as 'Everyone is being tested and you have to get things right now.' You only get one chance, so why not do it right? If you're a good person, you'll be prepared."

"Oh boy, I would need to brush up on my Bible verses for starters," says Richard Speight Jr. "If the Apocalypse came tomorrow, I think I'd be in deep doodoo. Maybe I'd just go shoot a porno and hope that somehow that would save me in the end. At least it'd be a nice souvenir for the people who were 'left behind'."

David Reed is prepared for that eventuality. "I actually have the 'zombie apocalypse' closet in my house that has the different implements, like an electric drill to drill the zombies' brains," he says. "You have to be thinking about these things." Of course, that closet is in his house, so what happens if a Zombie Apocalypse occurs while he's at the *Supernatural* offices? "We'd be screwed," says Rebecca Dessertine without hesitation. "Yeah, that actually would be pretty bad," Reed agrees. But the important question is, if zombies had everyone trapped in the *Supernatural* offices, in order to survive, who would Reed and Dessertine eat first? "We can't actually say,"

Above

Jensen Ackles on
location for 'The End'
on the *Supernatural*
backlot.

states Dessertine. "We have some people picked out," Reed explains.

"I wouldn't eat anyone!" Sera Gamble exclaims. "That's terrible!" Then she reconsiders. "I mean, unless I was a zombie, then whoever's closest, obviously, because my brain stem would be detached from my empathy center." Samantha Ferris empathizes with Gamble's initial response. "I couldn't eat a dead person," she insists. "I'd be the biggest wimp at the end of the world. I couldn't even eat my cat. I would rather drink a jug of booze and shoot myself in the head right before the big wave comes."

"I don't know what I'd do," says George Neuman. "I think I'd just grab a backpack and run for the hills." Samantha Smith would react similarly. "I think that if there was a real apocalypse, I would get out of Dodge really fast and go find some open piece of land where nobody could find me. I don't think it would be safe to be locked in a room somewhere," she muses, thinking about whether she should bother building a panic room like Bobby's in preparation for the end of times.

"Put the Jeep in four-wheel-drive, head for Montana, and pray for God's protection," Nicole Baer states matter-of-factly. Jensen Ackles agrees with the praying part. "I know what I would do," he says, "I would go home and I'd go to church with my family. That's probably what I should be doing normally…"

If you're not the praying type, and you don't have a good place to run or hide, Robert Singer, who says he will "probably be under a table somewhere," has the simplest advice of all: "Bend over and kiss your ass goodbye!"

22 Ways To Ditch Destiny
By Dean Winchester

1. "Just Say No" to being an angel condom.

2. War is not inevitable — you can cut it off at the knees... or in some cases, at the finger.

3. Don't fight destiny alone if you don't have to.

4. The future isn't set in stone — change what you were going to do today and you'll change tomorrow.

5. Don't tempt fate: if something is cursed, stay away from it.

6. I Believe the Hot Girls Are Our Future.

7. Don't gamble with your life. If you're going to play that game, you might as well invite a Reaper to sit at the table. Tell him to bring the pretzels.

8. Sometimes TV *is* like life — if you don't like what's coming up next, don't stay tuned, change the channel. Then go get some pie.

9. Don't believe everything you read (especially on the internet). Even a prophet's vision of the future is just fiction until it happens.

10. Always question destiny. Remember, we surprised Lucifer with the Colt, so anything's possible.

11. Don't listen to the voices inside your head. Listen to your gut. Unless your gut is telling you to eat people, in which case you're probably a rougarou, and if you listen to that voice then we'll have to kill you.

12. Don't make a deal with a demon unless you're prepared to put your heart into it. Literally.

13. Don't bother trying to change the past; focus on making sure there'll still be a future.

14. Don't suppress your hungers* – feed them regularly, in moderation, or else they'll be the death of you.

15. In case of a Zombie Apocalypse, always kill a zombie with a headshot.

16. The saying goes that "God helps those who help themselves" – and I have it on good authority that God doesn't think the Apocalypse is His problem – so it's up to everybody to fight the Apocalypse.

17. Beware false prophets. (And brothers who eat bean burritos. Gassy.)

18. If you're still breathing, it's not too late to change your mind.

19. Expect the unexpected. Sometimes the elephant in the room is really a vegan pagan god, and sometimes your enemy is really your ally.

20. If the enemy produces a hellhound, you produce a bigger hellhound.
    That's the *Winchester* way.

21. When Death comes for you, offer him some Chicago-style pizza – it might buy you some extra time (and if not, it still makes a pretty good last meal).

22. When all is said and done, if you're up against Destiny, make your own choice. (Hint: You can't go wrong if you choose humanity, and more specifically, family.)

*For the exception, see 11.

ALSO AVAILABLE FROM TITAN BOOKS

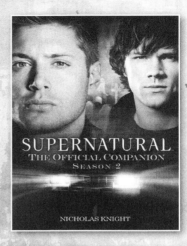

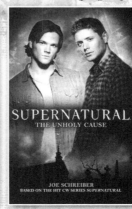

COMING 2011

MAY, JULY,
SEPTEMBER
3 ALL-NEW
SUPERNATURA
NOVELS

WWW.TITANBOOKS.COM